The Pedestal Philosophy

Your Pedestal. Your Power. Your Truth.

Dr. Pamela Gurley, D.M.

Clark and Hill Enterprise

First Printing, 2025

ISBN 979-8-9990790-1-5

Printed in the United States of America

Contents

Dedication

To my husband, Jay. Thank you for standing beside me, cheering me on, and being so patient with all that I ambitiously pursue. I am endlessly grateful for the joy, balance, and partnership you bring to my life. Your love is unlike anything I could have ever prayed for.

To my amazing mother, thank you for being my first teacher, my greatest supporter, and the foundation of my strength. Your love, wisdom, and resilience have shaped me into the woman I am today. Also, thank you for telling me to "write the book."

To my dad, thank you for your unconditional love and unwavering support. I am, and always will be, your angel and your Hollywood.

To my sisters, Ro, and Robin, as well as all of my nieces and nephews. I love every moment and memory I get to make with you all. #FamilyFirst

Foreword

From the moment I met Dr. Pamela Gurley, I sensed a woman who had not just survived life's storms but learned to dance in the rain. Her presence radiates the wisdom of someone who has faced adversity, transformed pain into power, and emerged with a voice that is both unflinching and compassionate. Dr. Gurley's journey is more than a story of trials and triumphs; it is a living testament to what it means to reclaim your worth and build a life on your own terms.

In these pages, you will find more than lessons. You will find lived experience—raw, honest, and unfiltered. *The Pedestal Philosophy* was not born in comfort but in the ashes of realignment and reassignment. Every scar, every setback, every victory has shaped the framework you now hold in your hands. Dr. Gurley's life is proof that your pedestal is not handed to you. It is forged, brick by brick, through courage, self-reflection, and relentless self-love.

As a psychotherapist, I know how often we carry invisible wounds—old stories of betrayal, disappointment, and self-doubt that keep us from seeing our true value. Dr. Gurley does not ask you to ignore your pain. Instead, she invites you to use it as fuel, to break free from self-limiting beliefs, and to craft a new narrative rooted in self-awareness and emotional wellness.

I have seen Dr. Gurley show up for others with the same devotion she gives herself. She will drive or fly across states, standing by her loved ones without hesitation. The authenticity she lives is the authenticity she offers you: practical, relatable, and fiercely empowering. She reminds us all that pedestals are not built from perfection, titles, or applause; they are built from truth, vulnerability, and the daily choice to honor your own journey.

After reading this book, I invite my clients, and now I invite you, to define your own pedestal. It is never too late to step up, to claim your space, and to discover the courage to be unapologetically yourself. This work is not easy. It asks you to confront your deepest fears and to let go of the need for external validation. But the reward is freedom—the freedom to live, love, and lead from a place of wholeness.

If you are holding this book, know that you are not alone. Let these lessons challenge you, heal you, and remind you that you are enough. Your pedestal is waiting. The only question is: will you rise to meet it?

With grace, light, and love,

Dr. Cortina D. Peters – Louis, Ph.D.

LMHC – QS, LPC, LCPC, CST

"The Girlfriend Therapist" ®

Psychotherapist. Author. Storyteller. Purpose Coach.

About the Author of the Foreword

Dr. Cortina Peters-Louis, affectionately known as "The Girlfriend Therapist," is a licensed mental health professional, speaker, and advocate for healing, authenticity, and inner freedom. With a heart for helping individuals reclaim their voice and value, she shows up with clinical insight and girlfriend-level realness. Dr. Peters just...gets it. Whether in the therapy room, on stage, or through her writing, she invites us to take up space, heal our wounds, and step confidently onto our own pedestal—no validation required.

Preface

When I published my first book, I *Am Not a Stereotype: I Am H.E.R.*, in 2019, I believed I was sharing the most authentic version of myself. Within its pages, I introduced the concept of *The Pedestal Philosophy*, a framework born from my experiences, observations, and the lessons life had taught me (psychologically called *Grounded Theory*). At the time, I thought a single chapter was enough to convey its significance. After all, how much more could I possibly say about it? I found healing by embracing it.

But life has a way of showing us just how much we do not know—about ourselves, about our journeys, and about the truths we *think* we have mastered. Shortly after the book's release, I was encouraged...no, I was told, that *The Pedestal Philosophy* needed to be more than just a chapter. It needed to stand on its own as a book. I resisted at first. Hell, I have pretty much resisted until now.

Writing about your personal life is an exhausting process that takes time, attention, care, *and* therapy. It requires you to dig deep, to confront your wounds, and to expose parts of yourself that you have carefully kept hidden. At that time, I did not think I had the capacity to give more.

What I did not realize then was that I was still evolving within the philosophy. I was still growing through it, still learning what it meant to truly sit on my own pedestal. I thought I was healed, and in many ways, I was. However, healing is not the same as living in complete alignment with your truth. I realized I was not yet fully living the life I had written about. I wanted things to look a certain way, to feel a certain way, to align with my expectations. But life rarely unfolds according to our expectations.

What I wanted from the Pedestal Philosophy and what it gave me were not the same—at least not initially. I thought I was offering the world a tool for living authentically, but what I received in return was a mirror, reflecting the parts of me that still needed work. I had to confront the disconnect between the life I envisioned and the life I was actually living. And while that disconnect did not dramatically disturb my life, it did force me to grow.

It has been five years since I first introduced *The Pedestal Philosophy* to the world, and in that time, it has transformed not just as a theoretical concept but as a way of life. It has shaped me in ways I could not have imagined. It has taught me to embrace my imperfections (especially as I have grown older), release my need for control while holding on to my choices, and live authentically in *every* aspect of my life.

This book is the result of that growth. It is not just an expansion of the ideas I introduced in 2019; it is a testament to the journey I have taken since then. It is a reflection of the lessons I have learned, the challenges I have overcome, the complacency I have given up, and the truths I have come to embody. I know it sounds cliché, but writing this book has been both an insightful privilege and a labor of love.

If you've ever felt unworthy, overlooked, or disconnected from your true self, this book is for you. It is an invitation to step into your power, reclaim your worth, and live a life that is unapologetically yours...*your truths*. It is my hope that the Pedestal

Philosophy will inspire you to build your own pedestal, sit firmly on it, and live authentically in the fullness of who you are. Welcome to what is now your journey and a continuum of mine.

Chapter 1

Introduction

What if the most significant turning point in your life was not a moment of triumph, but a moment of realization? What if the most radical act of self-love was not a grand gesture, but a quiet decision to see yourself—truly see yourself—for the first time? The Pedestal Philosophy was born from such a realization, and it is my invitation for you to experience your own.

We live in a world that constantly measures us. From early childhood, we are handed scripts about who we should be, how we should act, and what it means to succeed. We learn to chase approval, to strive for perfection, and to silence the parts of ourselves that do not fit the mold of what feels or seems like social norms. These lessons are reinforced everywhere: in schools, social media, television, movies, workplaces, rooted in certain cultures, family dynamics, and even in our closest personal relationships. The result is often a subtle, persistent sense of disconnection. A feeling that we are living a life that is not entirely our own. Or maybe, not ours at all.

The Pedestal Philosophy is a response to that disconnection. It is not a theory built from textbooks or academic research. It is not a collection of rules to memorize or a one-size-fits-all formula for happiness. Instead, it is a living practice, shaped by the raw, unfiltered experiences of real life. It is the wisdom that emerges from heartbreak, resilience, vulnerability, and the courage to begin again. This philosophy is about reclaiming your right to define yourself, honoring your needs, and building a life that feels authentic.

At its essence, the Pedestal Philosophy asks you to pause and ask: Whose pedestal am I standing on? Is it one built by others—by their expectations, their praise, their criticism? Or is it one you have constructed for yourself, based on your own values, dreams, and self-respect? The journey begins with this question, and it continues every day as you learn to listen to your intuition, trust your voice, and make choices that align with your truth.

You may wonder why this matters. Why not simply go along with what is expected, especially if it brings approval or comfort?

The answer is simple: because living on someone else's pedestal is always temporary and always fragile. The approval of others can be withdrawn at any moment. The standards you strive to meet may change without warning. When your sense of self is built on external validation, you are at the mercy of forces beyond your control. Over time, this erodes your confidence, your joy, and your sense of purpose.

The Pedestal Philosophy is about building something lasting. It is about creating a foundation of self-worth that is not dependent on the shifting sands of other people's opinions. It is about learning to celebrate your strengths, honor your boundaries, and accept your imperfections. This is not an act of arrogance or isolation. On the contrary, it is the foundation for deeper connection, greater compassion, and more authentic relationships.

Throughout this book, you will encounter stories—some my own and some interactions I have heard from others—about the messy, beautiful, and sometimes painful process of stepping onto your own pedestal. These stories are not meant to be prescriptive. You will not find a checklist or a ten-step plan. Instead, you will find reflections, questions, and invitations to explore your own journey. The Pedestal Philosophy is not about arriving at a destination. It is about learning to walk your path with intention, courage, and grace.

One of the most important lessons of this philosophy is that self-worth is not a static state. It is something you cultivate, nurture, and protect. There will be days when you feel strong and confident, and days when you feel lost and unsure. Both are part of the journey. The pedestal is not a place you reach, and it stays the same forever. It is a space you reevaluate again and again, building through the life lessons—especially when life feels overwhelming or uncertain.

You may encounter resistance from within and from the world around you. Old habits and beliefs may whisper that you are not enough, that you must keep performing, pleasing, or achieving to deserve love. Some people may even resent your decision to prioritize your well-being, especially if they are used to you putting their needs first. The Pedestal Philosophy does not promise that the path will be easy. What it does promise is that the rewards are real: a more profound sense of peace, a clearer sense of purpose, and a life that is your own.

This book is not just about individual transformation. It is about collective change. When you choose to honor your worth and live authentically, you give others permission to do the same. You become a beacon for those who are struggling to find their voice. You create ripples that extend far beyond your own life—into your family, your community, and the world at large. The Pedestal Philosophy is not just a personal practice; it is a movement toward greater self-respect, compassion, and empowerment for all.

You may be wondering where to begin. The truth is you have already started simply by picking up this book. The desire to reconnect with your true self, to step out of the shadows of others' expectations, is the first and most important step. As you read, I invite you to approach each chapter with curiosity and openness. You do not have to agree with everything you find here. You do not have to follow every suggestion. The Pedestal Philosophy is about discovering what resonates with you and having the courage to let go of what does not.

You will encounter questions designed to help you reflect on your journey. Take your time with them. You can write in the margins, pause to think, or discuss them with someone you trust. The work of building your own pedestal is deeply personal, and there is no right or wrong way to do it. Trust yourself to know what you need, not need it just because it is written here.

As you navigate these pages, you may also encounter moments of discomfort. Growth often requires us to confront parts of ourselves that we have kept hidden or neglected. You may realize that you have been living by someone else's script, or that you have silenced your dreams for the sake of peace. These realizations can be painful, but they are also the doorway to freedom. The Pedestal Philosophy invites you to meet yourself with compassion, to forgive your past, extend yourself lots of grace, and to choose a new way forward.

This book is not about perfection. It is about progress. It is about making the choice, day after day, to return to your pedestal, to honor your truth, and to live with intention. There will be setbacks, and that is to be expected. The goal is not to never fall, but to always rise again, and do so wiser, stronger, and more compassionate with yourself.

In the chapters ahead, you will find stories of resilience, tools for self-reflection, and reminders that you are not alone. You will be invited to define your own values, set boundaries that honor your needs, and celebrate the unique strengths you bring to the world. The Pedestal Philosophy is not about separating yourself from others, but about connecting more deeply with yourself, with those you love, and with the world around you.

As you begin this journey, I encourage you to let go of the need for approval, the pressure to be perfect, and the fear of disappointing others. Give yourself permission to be fully, unapologetically you. Build your pedestal with intention, stand on it with courage, and know that you are worthy of every good thing life has to offer.

This is your invitation. This is your moment. The Pedestal Philosophy is no longer just an idea or a chapter in my previous book. It is a living, breathing practice that you are now open to being a part of.

Let us begin.

Chapter 2

The Foundation of the Pedestal

If you did not read my first book, I Am Not a Stereotype: I Am H.E.R., released in 2019, you are now invited into the whole foundation of what I call the *Pedestal Philosophy*. Unlike frameworks rooted in research or data, this philosophy is born from personal observation, lived experience, and the challenging, sometimes painful, lessons life brings. It is a perspective that, once internalized, unlocks a deeper understanding of self-worth and self-love. At its heart, the Pedestal Philosophy is about the universal desire to be elevated, cherished, and valued. However, while we often seek to be placed on someone else's pedestal, we frequently neglect the most vital pedestal of all: our own.

What does it mean to place yourself on your own pedestal? The value is immeasurable. When you love yourself enough to elevate your own worth, you liberate yourself from the exhausting chase for external validation. Your focus naturally shifts toward your own expectations, your happiness, and your sense of peace. Some may call this selfish, but it is, in fact, essential. True comfort and joy are found within. That inner satisfaction begins with listening to your intuition, honoring your spirit, and prioritizing your self-worth.

This concept is powerfully reflected in Maslow's hierarchy of needs, a foundational theory of human motivation. Maslow (1943) proposed that self-actualization, the highest level of psychological development, can only be achieved after foundational needs such as love, belonging, and self-esteem are met. The Pedestal Philosophy aligns with this by emphasizing self-love and self-esteem as prerequisites for personal growth. When you fully accept yourself and meet your own emotional needs, you create a foundation for thriving, unlocking the possibility of fulfilling your highest potential.

This is not a philosophy of isolation or withdrawal. In fact, embracing self-love and authenticity makes you more compassionate, less judgmental, and better equipped to care for others. When you build your own pedestal, you show up as a better listener, friend, partner, and parent. The balance between loving yourself and loving others is where authenticity flourishes. You can give without depleting yourself, and in doing so, you become a source of inspiration and support for those around you.

Consider the fundamental question: What am I truly worth? The answer should be a glowing list of intangible qualities that reflect your value. If you struggle to answer, it is time to pause and reflect. What is holding you back from living in alignment with your worth? Whose life are you living if not your own? Are you fulfilled? When you place yourself on your pedestal, these questions become easier to answer with honesty and clarity.

I have not always known what it means to truly honor my own worth. For a long time, I moved through life measuring myself by the standards and desires of others. I found myself in relationships that chipped away at my confidence, where I became so focused on being what someone else needed that I lost sight of who I was. There were seasons when I convinced myself that if I could just be more accommodating, more patient, or more "enough," I would finally be loved the way I longed for. However, each time I ignored a red flag or silenced my own needs, I felt less visible to myself.

There was a point when I looked in the mirror and barely recognized the woman staring back. I realized I had spent years shrinking, apologizing, and contorting myself to fit into someone else's idea of love and acceptance. The pain of losing myself, of feeling invisible in my own story, became heavier than the fear of letting go. It was in that vulnerable moment that I asked myself a simple but life-changing question: What if I stopped waiting for someone to choose me, and instead chose myself?

That was the beginning of my journey back to myself. I started to notice the small ways I had abandoned my own happiness: the hobbies I gave up, the boundaries I let slide, the dreams I put on hold. I made a conscious decision to reclaim those parts of me, to nurture my interests, and to speak my truth, even if my voice trembled. It was not about building walls or shutting people out; it was about building a foundation strong enough to support my own growth.

I also began to reflect on the qualities I brought to relationships, not just what I hoped to receive, but what I offered. I wrote out the values that mattered most to me and made a promise never to compromise them for the sake of belonging. In doing so, I discovered a new kind of freedom: the freedom to be fully myself, regardless of who stayed or left.

Life, even in its pain, holds beauty. I have experienced joy, heartbreak, resilience, and moments where I lost myself in others. I have ignored red flags, compromised my happiness, and lived for someone else. Today, my pedestal belongs to me. It does not make me immune to pain or life's challenges, but it gives me a sense of stability and confidence. No matter what happens or who leaves, my happiness remains intact because it is rooted in me. Here, William James's concept of self-esteem provides a valuable lens. James (1890) suggested that the ratio of our successes to our aspirations determines self-esteem. When we set realistic, attainable goals that are genuinely our own, we build confidence and avoid the emotional toll of chasing standards that do not fit us. The Pedestal Philosophy, in this way, encourages you to accept your imperfections and set goals that honor your actual capacity, not the unrealistic standards set by others or by society. This keeps you grounded, focused, and free from the trap of self-discrepancy.

The process of self-love is not automatic; it is a daily practice that requires dedication. It requires effort, reflection, and a commitment to prioritize your own joy and comfort. Authenticity means knowing and accepting every part of who you are. Self-love means favoring your happiness and well-being over the need to please others. This does not mean you never compromise in relationships, but it does mean you never compromise your self-respect, values, or peace.

The early stages of a relationship often feel intoxicating. We all crave to be cherished and admired. However, where does this admiration lead? Too often, we fight to be placed on a pedestal of someone else's creation instead of building our own. This is a question worth reflecting on. There are pivotal moments in life, especially during the time between heartbreak and rediscovering yourself, that shape personal growth. If you have ever loved someone so deeply that you lost yourself, you know how challenging it is to reclaim your sense of self. I have been there. I have ignored toxicity, forgiven the unforgivable, and fought for relationships that were breaking me and broke me. Eventually, I prayed, listened to my spirit, and let go of what was unhealthy and unchanging. It was the hardest, but most necessary, decision.

The Sociometer Theory, developed by Leary and colleagues (1995), suggests that self-esteem is a gauge, or "sociometer," that tracks our social standing and sense of belonging. While social connections are important, not all relationships are healthy. Toxic relationships can erode self-esteem and make us doubt our worth. The Pedestal Philosophy encourages you to nurture relationships that uplift and support you while maintaining a strong sense of self-reliance. It is about being selective with your connections and prioritizing those that reflect and reinforce your values.

This process was not linear or easy for me. There were setbacks, moments of doubt, and times when old patterns tried to pull me back into familiar, but unhealthy, territory. However, with each conscious choice to honor my needs and respect my boundaries, I felt my confidence and sense of self-worth grow stronger. I learned that my pedestal is not a place of perfection or superiority; it is a space of authenticity, healing, and self-respect. Now, when I think about what it means to sit on my own pedestal, I remember how far I have come. I know that my value does not depend on validation from anyone else. My happiness, peace, and power are mine to claim and protect. I am my own safe space. And that, more than anything, is the foundation that allows me to show up for others from a place of abundance, not depletion.

Rebuilding self-love can feel like searching through a lost-and-found for your own growth. I was emotionally scattered but knew I needed to take control. I began by making two lists: one of things I genuinely enjoy without fear or judgment, and another of the qualities I bring to a relationship. The first list reminded me who I was apart from others. The second helped define my worth and what I deserved in a partner. Through these lists, I learned to focus on qualities of substance and let go of superficial expectations. Self-love requires balance and humility. You cannot demand qualities from others that you do not embody yourself. If you respect yourself, you will not tolerate disrespect from others. If you desire certain qualities, work on cultivating them within yourself.

This aligns with Self-Determination Theory, which highlights the importance of autonomy, competence, and relatedness for personal growth (Deci & Ryan, 1985). According to this theory, people thrive when they feel a sense of control over their lives, believe in their own abilities, and experience meaningful connections. By focusing on your needs and strengths, you build a life that is fulfilling and true to yourself. You stop relying on external validation for happiness and begin to flourish authentically.

Growth, I have discovered, is not about avoiding pain but about learning and healing through it. Growth means living intentionally and letting go of idle "what ifs." It is about embracing the satisfaction that comes from trying, even if you do not always succeed. Each attempt to honor your worth, each step toward your own pedestal, strengthens your foundation.

It is important to recognize that placing yourself on your pedestal is not a one-time act. It is an ongoing process, a commitment to return to yourself again and again. There will be setbacks, moments of self-doubt, and times when you feel pulled back onto someone else's pedestal. The key is persistence and self-compassion. Neff (2003) describes self-compassion as treating yourself with kindness and understanding, especially when you fall short of your ideals. When you stumble, remember that you are practicing a new way of being. Give yourself grace and keep moving forward.

The Pedestal Philosophy also recognizes the importance of boundaries. Setting boundaries is a way of protecting your energy and values. It is not about shutting people out, but about creating space for your own needs to be met. Boundaries can be as simple as carving out time for rest, declining a social invitation, or communicating your limits at work or in relationships. Each time you set a boundary, you reinforce your right to exist on your own terms.

As you continue to build and strengthen your pedestal, you will notice changes not only in yourself but also in your relationships and environment. When you stand firmly in your own worth, you inspire others to do the same. The Pedestal Philosophy recognizes that empowered individuals create empowered communities. Your courage to honor yourself becomes a silent invitation for others to reflect on where they have given away their own power and how they might reclaim it.

Practical steps can help anchor this philosophy in your life. Start by reflecting on where and to whom you have given your power away. Identify the beliefs or relationships that keep you from living fully. Practice saying no, even when it feels uncomfortable. Celebrate every moment you choose yourself, no matter how small. Surround yourself with people who encourage your autonomy and growth.

Most importantly, give yourself permission to build and climb onto your own pedestal. Life will always present challenges, critics, and distractions, but your power remains yours to reclaim. The world does not benefit from your shrinking. It is transformed when you stand tall, rooted in the truth that you are enough.

Reclaiming your pedestal, through the lens of the Pedestal Philosophy, is about coming home to yourself. It is about honoring your journey, trusting your intuition, and living as if your life belongs to you, because it does. Let this be your invitation to step boldly onto your own pedestal, not just for a moment, but for a lifetime.

Now it is your turn. Take a moment to reflect, make your own lists, and create the life you deserve. This is your life. Live it authentically, love it fiercely, and embrace it unapologetically. Sitting on your pedestal is not about arrogance; it is about honoring your worth and living your truth. The transformation it brings is real. So, LIVE your truth. LOVE your life. EMBRACE your journey. That is what it means to sit on YOUR pedestal.

Chapter 3

Loving Yourself First

L oving yourself first is more than an abstract idea; it is a daily practice and a conscious commitment to prioritizing your emotional, mental, and spiritual well-being. At its core, loving yourself first means recognizing that the most important relationship you will ever have is the one you have with yourself. This is not about selfishness. It is about survival, about laying the foundation for a life where joy and fulfillment are possible.

There is a unique strength that comes from nurturing self-love. It is not simply about feeling good or boosting your mood. It is about creating a stable foundation for every other area of your life. When you genuinely love yourself, you stop waiting for others to validate your worth or permit yourself to be authentic. You begin to show up for yourself in ways that feel empowering and deeply satisfying. Self-love becomes the anchor that grounds you, regardless of what is happening around you.

Reflecting on my own journey, I realize how much time I spent in my early adulthood trying to meet the expectations of others. Whether in my career, relationships, or even in how I presented myself, I was constantly seeking approval. I wanted to be seen as successful, capable, and strong. However, in the process of molding myself to fit other people's ideals, I lost sight of who I truly wanted to be. The signs were subtle at first: agreeing to things I did not want, overextending myself to prove I was enough, and pushing through exhaustion to avoid disappointing others. I thought I was doing the right thing, but instead, I was neglecting my own needs and values, and ultimately, my sense of self. This was the period in my life when I found myself saying "yes" out of obligation rather than genuine desire. I would sign up for nonprofit boards, take on extra projects at work, or attend social events even when my body and spirit were begging for rest.

I remember several times when my calendar was packed with commitments, yet I felt utterly exhausted and empty. I was so focused on being dependable for others that I became undependable for myself. My needs were always the last to be considered, and I wore my exhaustion like a badge of honor. A

During my undergraduate studies in psychology, I remember reading about William James's self-esteem formula: success divided by pretensions (James, 1890). Looking back, I realized that I had set impossibly high expectations for myself, driven by a desire for external validation. At this time in my life, I did not pause; I overcompensated to avoid dealing with the discomfort of feeling inadequate. I believed that if I just accomplished enough, I could quiet that persistent sense of falling short. However, the more I achieved, the more disconnected I felt from my own desires and needs. I was constantly falling short in my own eyes.

James's theory offers a powerful reminder: self-esteem grows when we set realistic goals that are aligned with who we are, not who others want us to be. When we recalibrate our aspirations to reflect our true selves, we begin to experience genuine confidence and satisfaction.

This insight also connects directly to Maslow's Hierarchy of Needs, which highlights the importance of love and self-esteem as prerequisites for reaching self-actualization (Maslow, 1943). According to Maslow, self-love is not optional. It is the bridge to becoming the best version of ourselves. When we prioritize our own emotional needs, we create the conditions for growth, creativity, and fulfillment.

For me, the turning point came when I realized that my life was filled with activities and obligations that did not reflect what I truly wanted or needed. I had become so accustomed to living for others that I had forgotten how to live for myself. This realization brought an overwhelming sense of emptiness, not because my life was lacking, but because it was not enough of my own. I could have said "not my own;" however, the reality of experiencing life is trying new things you are invited to do (especially if it sounds exciting). Nevertheless, loving myself first became a necessity. It took sitting alone, feeling numb and disconnected, for me to realize that something had to change. That moment was a quiet awakening; a reminder that I could not pour from an empty cup.

I had to place boundaries on what I thought I should do because someone else wanted to do it. I also had to stop waiting for others to validate my worth in how I spent my time and start showing up authentically for myself. I learned to become my own safe space, my own biggest cheerleader, and my own voice. While support from others is valuable, it is impossible to truly benefit from it if you are disconnected from your own needs.

Sometimes, loving yourself first means making choices that others do not understand. I recall a time when I stepped back from a long-standing friendship that had become one-sided and emotionally draining. The decision was not easy, and it was met with confusion and even criticism from those around me. Nevertheless, I knew that holding on out of guilt or habit was costing me my peace. By letting go, I created room for relationships that were reciprocal and nourishing. It was a valuable lesson in discernment. A reminder that self-love sometimes means walking away from what no longer serves your growth.

Kristin Neff's self-compassion theory became a guiding light during this process. Neff (2003) emphasizes the importance of treating yourself with kindness and understanding, especially during moments of failure or difficulty. Loving myself first required that I offer myself the same grace I extended to others. I had to embrace my imperfections and learn to view myself with compassion instead of criticism.

The process was far from easy. Years of putting others before myself had to be unlearned. Setting boundaries felt uncomfortable, and saying "no" brought guilt. I began to carve out time for the things that brought me joy—writing, traveling, cooking, and simply being present with myself. I started asking myself what I needed, and for the first time, genuinely listened to the answer. This practice echoes the Self-Determination Theory, which highlights autonomy, competence, and relatedness as essential for personal growth (Deci & Ryan, 1985). By tuning into my needs and taking action to fulfill them, I reclaimed my autonomy and began to build a life rooted in intrinsic motivation and joy.

With time, I saw that loving myself first was not just for me; it was the key to transforming my relationship with the world around me. When you prioritize your well-being, you not only strengthen your relationship with yourself, but you also show up more authentically and intentionally in your interactions with others. You become lighter, freer, and more aligned with your truth. You develop discernment, which enables you to recognize and disentangle yourself from toxic relationships that drain you, making room for connections that uplift and support your growth.

The Sociometer Theory, proposed by Leary and colleagues (1995), explains how the quality of our relationships influences our self-esteem. We often do not realize how much our self-esteem is shaped by those whose opinions we value. By practicing discernment, I learned to surround myself with people (particularly women) who aligned with my values and contributed to my growth, rather than those who diminished my light or resented it.

In choosing myself, I reclaimed my power. There is no greater freedom than this: prioritizing your emotional, mental, and spiritual well-being without hesitation. It is about embracing every part of who you are—the good, the messy, the imperfect, and even the parts that are still growing.

Loving yourself is a process that requires patience, reflection, and a commitment to your happiness. Once you begin, you will see how it transforms not only your relationship with yourself, but also the way you connect with the world. There will be moments of guilt and self-doubt, and times when you question whether prioritizing yourself is the right thing to do. Each time, remind yourself that loving you does not take away from others; it allows you to give them the best version of who you are. Loving myself first did not just change my life—it saved it.

Chapter 4
The Art of Self-Discovery

For years, I prided myself on being an achiever. I poured everything I had into my academics and career, chasing milestone after milestone, believing that success was the ultimate measure of my worth. On the outside, I appeared to have it all together—degrees, accolades, and professional accomplishments—but on the inside, I was toxic. I was so busy pouring into everything else (my work, my goals, my responsibilities) that I completely neglected to pour into myself.

I ignored my heart, my personal well-being, and the quiet voice inside me that kept asking, "What about you?" Of course, for years, I did not listen. I often outright ignored that quiet voice inside. I told myself that if I just worked harder, achieved more, and met everyone else's expectations, I would eventually feel whole.

Spoiler alert: that moment never came. No matter how much I achieved, it was never enough to fill the emptiness I felt inside.

I remember like it was yesterday, the moment it all caught up to me in what felt like a heavy swoop (or, dare I say, more like a hard kick in the ass) after realizing how many red flags I had ignored before and after my third marriage, and how I had to rebuild my life over for the THIRD time. I just broke down. I was not crying because I was overwhelmed by the work ahead of me. I was crying because I realized I no longer knew what made me happy. I had spent so much time being everything to everyone else that I had forgotten how to be anything to myself. I had neglected my own needs, my own joy, and my own peace. I compromised it all. What a tough pill to swallow. Even more so, what a helluva realization I had to heal from. Sometimes we need a hard wake-up for discovery to happen. And that moment was my turning point.

I realized that no amount of external success could ever make up for the lack of love I was showing myself. I had to start prioritizing myself, not as an afterthought, but as the foundation of everything I did. It was not easy. I had to learn how to say no, set boundaries, and give myself permission to just... be. I had to remind myself that my worth was not tied to my productivity or my achievements but to who I was at my core. I had A LOT to UNLEARN. Choosing yourself does not mean abandoning your goals or responsibilities. It means making yourself a priority in a world that constantly demands more from you. It is about realizing that you cannot be everything to everybody.

Kristin Neff's Self-Compassion Theory became a guiding light for me during this process. The theory emphasizes treating yourself with kindness and understanding, especially during moments of failure or difficulty (Neff, 2003). Self-compassion allowed me to confront the inner critic that had been driving me to exhaustion. It taught me to embrace my imperfections, acknowledge my pain, and give myself the grace to heal.

By practicing self-compassion, I began to reconnect with myself. I started asking, What makes me happy? What brings me peace? What do I need to feel whole? For the first time in years, I actually listened to the answers.

I realized that success is not just about accomplishments, accolades, or the approval of others. True success is about alignment. It is living a life that reflects your values, honors your needs, and brings you joy. This perspective aligns with Maslow's concept of self-actualization, the pinnacle of his Hierarchy of Needs (Maslow, 1943). Self-actualization is about realizing your full potential, but this can only happen when your foundational needs, such as love, belonging, and self-esteem, are met.

For me, self-discovery was about rebuilding those foundations. I had to create a sense of love and belonging within myself rather than seeking it from external sources. I had to redefine my self-esteem, rooting it in who I was rather than what I achieved.

One of the most transformative lessons I learned during this journey was the power of saying no. For years, I had been a people-pleaser, saying yes to everything and everyone, even when it came at the expense of my own well-being. I realized that every time I said yes to something that did not serve me, I was saying no to myself.

Saying no became an act of self-care. It allowed me to set boundaries, protect my peace, and prioritize what truly mattered. It was not about shutting people out—it was about making space for myself.

When you take care of yourself, you show up better in every area of your life. You are more present, more fulfilled, and more aligned with the life you deserve.

This idea is supported by Self-Determination Theory, which emphasizes the importance of autonomy, competence, and relatedness in achieving personal growth and fulfillment (Deci & Ryan, 1985). By prioritizing myself, I reclaimed my autonomy. I began making decisions based on what felt right to me rather than what others expected of me. I started pursuing goals that were meaningful to me, not just impressive to others.

Rebuilding my life was not easy, but it was necessary. I had to let go of the idea that my worth was tied to my achievements and embrace the truth that my worth was inherent. I had to stop living for others and start living for myself.

Self-discovery is not a one-time event; it is a lifelong journey. It requires you to continuously reflect, reassess, and realign with your truth (and being honest when that truth changes). The rewards are immeasurable. When you prioritize yourself, you create a life that is rich, meaningful, and deeply fulfilling.

Let this chapter serve as a reminder that it is never too late to rediscover yourself. It is never too late to prioritize your needs, honor your truth, and build a life that reflects who you truly are.

Chapter 5

Authenticity and Inner Validation

What does it really mean to live authentically? In today's world, "authenticity" is often tossed around as a buzzword, yet its depth is rarely explored. Authenticity is not about projecting an idealized version of yourself, nor is it about perfection. At its core, authenticity is about alignment. An alignment between who you are on the inside and how you show up in the world.

Living authentically encourages you to release masks and societal expectations. It involves choosing to live in a way that reflects your true self, even when that self is messy, complicated, broke, broken, hurt, grieving, or in flux. However, many people struggle to live authentically due to a fear of judgment, rejection, or failure. The desire for acceptance can be intense and often causes us to seek validation from others, hoping their approval confirms our worth. The pain of judgment and rejection is deepest when it comes from those we love. I understand this struggle personally because, for much of my life, I was caught in it too.

For years, I felt pressure to meet a standard of perfection—one that, in hindsight, I realize I helped create. I am not afraid to hold myself accountable for the ways I tried to control my image. I wanted to be loved and admired, but the reality was that my life behind the scenes was anything but perfect. My "mess" included marrying more than once despite my intuition telling me otherwise, staying in unhealthy relationships out of shame, facing family and friends who warned me I was making mistakes, and overcompensating with work and education to present a different image to the world. My achievements were admired, but my personal life felt unseen and unsupported. It was only when I paused, stepped back, and took time to heal that I began to see the truth: I was hiding my real life from the world and living for others, not for myself.

Healing taught me that inner validation is the key to authenticity. True authenticity cannot exist without accepting your truths, affirming your worth, trusting your voice, and honoring your experiences without needing external approval. Without inner validation, authenticity becomes fragile and easily influenced by others' opinions and expectations. When we develop inner validation, we gain the freedom to live a genuine, fulfilling, and uniquely our own life.

The Shame of Imperfection

One of the biggest obstacles to authenticity is the shame associated with imperfection. Society teaches us that to earn love, respect, or success, we must aim for flawlessness. We are urged to hide our vulnerabilities, not to reveal how we overcome our failures, and to always present a polished, put-together image. This culture of perfectionism fosters a deep shame in anyone who feels they fall short—and honestly, that's all of us at some point.

Shame whispers that our imperfections make us unworthy. It urges us to hide parts of ourselves we fear others will judge or reject. It drives us to craft our lives, perform for acceptance, and meet others' expectations. However, the truth is that shame is misleading. It thrives in secrecy and silence, feeding on our insecurities and preventing us from living authentically.

When shame controls our lives, we disconnect from our true selves. We focus so heavily on meeting outside expectations that we lose sight of what truly matters to us. We stop listening to our intuition, neglect our needs, and stray from our unique paths. Over time, this disconnection results in emptiness, dissatisfaction, and resentment. We may attain success by society's standards, but without authenticity, that success feels hollow.

The antidote to shame is self-compassion. Kristin Neff's Self-Compassion Theory suggests that treating ourselves with kindness and understanding, especially during moments of failure or imperfection, is essential for personal growth (Neff, 2003). Self-compassion helps us face shame directly, accept our flaws without judgment, and embrace our humanity. When we practice self-compassion, we lay the groundwork for inner validation, which in turn supports our ability to live authentically.

Authenticity as a Gateway to Inner Freedom

Authenticity is not just about being honest with others; it is about being honest with yourself too. It requires confronting and accepting the parts of yourself you've been taught to hide. It means embracing your vulnerabilities and living in line with your true self. This is not easy. It takes courage to let go of needing external approval and to trust that you are enough just as you are.

Living authentically means allowing yourself to be imperfect. It involves understanding that your worth is not connected to your ego, achievements, appearance, or meeting others' expectations. Your worth is intrinsic. It comes from your humanity, experiences, and your unique perspective on the world. It involves understanding that your worth is not connected to your ego, achievements, appearance, or meeting others' expectations. Your worth is intrinsic. It comes from your humanity, experiences, and your unique perspective on the world.

Brené Brown, a prominent researcher on shame and vulnerability, defines authenticity as "the daily practice of letting go of who we think we are supposed to be and embracing who we are" (Brown, 2012). This practice is freeing because it releases you from the constant pressure to perform. It enables you to show up as your whole self, flaws and all, and to find joy in simply being. When you no longer feel the need to prove your worth to others, you become free to live a life that is true to you, not one driven by others' expectations.

Maslow's Hierarchy of Needs also offers a helpful framework for understanding the link between authenticity and fulfillment. At the top of the hierarchy is self-actualization—the realization of one's full potential. According to Maslow (1943), self-actualization is only possible when the basic needs of love, belonging, and self-esteem are met. Authenticity and inner validation are essential for satisfying these needs. When you validate yourself from within, you build self-esteem rooted in your true self. As a result, you gain the ability to live a life that truly aligns with your values, morals, and goals.

The Role of Inner Validation

Do you truly trust yourself? I mean, really trust your own instincts because developing inner validation involves learning to believe in yourself. It means acknowledging that your feelings, needs, and desires are valid, even if they do not match what others expect or want from you. This change is transformative. It enables you to pursue goals that matter to you, to build relationships that support your growth, and to make choices that stay true to you.

Self-determination theory, developed by Edward Deci and Richard Ryan, highlights the importance of autonomy, competence, and relatedness in achieving personal fulfillment (Deci & Ryan, 1985). Autonomy is the ability to make choices that reflect your values, which is a key part of inner validation. When you validate yourself from within, you take ownership of your life. This sense of autonomy lays the groundwork for fulfillment, enabling you to live a life that is true to who you are.

Inner validation also involves learning to recognize whose feedback and opinions genuinely matter. Not all criticism is helpful, and not all praise is significant. Relying only on external validation makes you vulnerable to the unpredictable fluctuations of others' opinions. Developing inner validation allows you to evaluate feedback through the perspective of your own values and goals. You pay attention to those who truly care about your growth and well-being, but you do not let their voices drown out your own.

Practical Steps Toward Authenticity and Inner Validation

Embracing authenticity and building inner validation is a lifelong journey, not a final goal. It demands daily effort, self-awareness, and a readiness to be vulnerable. Here are some practical steps that can help keep this practice rooted in your life.

Practice Self-Reflection: Dedicate regular time to thinking about your thoughts, feelings, and experiences. Journaling can help you recognize patterns, clarify your values, and monitor your growth over time.

1. Set Boundaries: Learn to say no to things that do not serve you, even if it disappoints others. Boundaries are crucial for protecting your energy and respecting your needs.

2. Embrace your imperfections: Practice self-compassion when you make mistakes or fall short of your ideals. Remind yourself that imperfection is part of being human.

3. Align Your Actions with Your Values: Make choices that reflect what matters most to you, rather than what is expected by others. This alignment is the core of authenticity.

4. Seek Support: Surround yourself with people who encourage your growth and support your journey toward authenticity. Community can provide strength and accountability.

5. Celebrate Your Progress: Recognize the steps you take toward living authentically, no matter how small. Progress matters more than perfection.

The Rewards of Authentic Living

When you embrace authenticity and inner validation, you open the door to a life that's rich, meaningful, and deeply fulfilling. You release the burden of shame and the need for external approval. You become more resilient when facing criticism and more compassionate toward yourself and others. You find a sense of peace that comes from living in alignment with your truth.

Most importantly, you give yourself permission to live imperfectly and fully. You embrace the journey, with all its ups and downs, and trust that you are enough just as you are. Your imperfections are not weaknesses; they are part of what makes you unique. Honor them, learn from them, and let them guide you toward a life of authenticity and inner peace.

Authenticity is a continuous practice, not a final destination. Inner validation is not something you automatically get; it is a gift you give yourself every day. When you choose to live authentically and validate yourself from within, you become the author of your own story. That, more than anything, is what it means to live a life

that is truly yours.

Chapter 6

Shattering the Illusion of the Pedestal

There is an undeniable appeal to being placed on someone else's pedestal. At first, it feels like an honor—a validation of your worth and a public acknowledgment of your value. The admiration, the approval, the feeling of being truly seen and appreciated can be intoxicating. It is easy to get caught up in the glow of being chosen, of being set apart. Beneath that surface lies a truth that is often overlooked: external pedestals are illusions, fragile by design, and ultimately unsustainable.

For a long time, I believed that being admired meant I was doing something right. Whether in relationships, at work, or in the way I presented myself to the world, I equated admiration with acceptance and success. I thought that as long as I stayed on someone else's pedestal, I was safe and valued. Over time, I began to notice the cracks beneath my feet. The pedestal was not stable because it was never mine to begin with. It was built from the expectations, ideals, and insecurities of others. The more I tried to stay balanced on it, the more I lost touch with my own truth, especially in my closest relationships.

The real danger became evident the moment I failed to meet someone's expectations. Suddenly, the pedestal I had been on felt unstable, even hostile. I saw how risky it is to depend on others for validation and happiness. In seeking approval, I had surrendered my power, and in doing so, I lost track of who I was. This kind of awakening is painful but essential. It forced me to face the truth that I could no longer stand on pedestals that were not mine. I needed to step down and start building my own.

The Fragility of External Pedestals

External pedestals can be tempting because they seem to offer a quick way to feel worthy. When someone places you on theirs, it feels like you have been chosen, like you are special. This validation is always conditional. It depends on their perception, standards, and ever-changing opinions. If you fail to meet those standards or if their perception shifts, you risk being knocked down.

This is the inherent risk of external pedestals: they are unstable because they are not rooted in your truth. They are built from what others believe you should be, not from who you truly are. Relying on external validation to determine your worth makes you vulnerable to rejection, criticism, and even emotional or mental harm. Your self-esteem becomes a reflection of others' opinions instead of an expression of your genuine self.

Sociometer Theory provides a strong explanation for this dynamic. According to Leary and colleagues (1995), our self-esteem is closely connected to how we perceive social inclusion or exclusion. We are wired to seek belonging and acceptance, but when we rely too much on others' approval, our sense of self-worth can become fragile. The more external sources influence our value, the more likely we are to feel unworthy when those sources withdraw their support.

The Illusion of Stability

External validation often creates an illusion of stability. It feels reassuring to be admired and told that you are enough. This sense of security is temporary. The more you rely on others to determine your worth, the greater your risk of disappointment and self-doubt. You might find yourself shaping your identity to match someone else's ideals, losing sight of your own needs and desires in the process.

William James's idea of self-esteem offers helpful insight here. James (1890) described self-esteem as the ratio of success to aspirations. When others control your aspirations, you set yourself up for ongoing dissatisfaction. External standards are often impossible to reach, inconsistent, or constantly changing. As a result, you may always feel inadequate, even while trying to meet those expectations. Genuine self-esteem, instead, is built by setting goals that align with your own values and abilities—goals grounded in your truth rather than someone else's idea of who you should be.

The pedestal created by others cannot support your authenticity. It is meant to hold an image of you that matches their expectations, not your true self. When you show parts of yourself that do not fit their ideals, the pedestal begins to crack. When it finally falls, you are left questioning your worth—not because you lack value, but because you let someone else define it for you.

Breaking Free from the Illusion

Realizing that you are living for others instead of yourself can be both painful and liberating. It makes you confront tough questions: Whose expectations am I following? What do I really want? What makes me feel whole? Most importantly, how can I build a life that shows my truth, not someone else's?

For years, I was my own harshest critic, comparing myself to others' standards. I absorbed their opinions, believing my worth relied on their approval. As I started practicing self-compassion, I learned to accept my imperfections and see myself with kindness. Kristin Neff's self-compassion theory highlights the importance of treating yourself with understanding and care, especially during times of failure or difficulty (Neff, 2003). This change helped me let go of the need for constant external validation and focus on building a foundation of self-love.

Self-compassion does not mean ignoring feedback or refusing to grow. It means understanding that you deserve love and respect, even when you do not meet others' or your own expectations. It involves giving yourself permission to be imperfect and to learn from your experiences without being overly harsh on yourself.

Moving Forward

If you feel drawn to external praise, take a moment to pause and reflect. Ask yourself whose approval you are seeking and why. Consider what it means to prioritize your own needs, values, and well-being. Be compassionate with yourself when you stumble and remember that growth is a journey, not a final destination.

Surround yourself with people who appreciate your authenticity and support your growth. Choose relationships that are supportive and mutual, not conditional or controlling. Remember, the quality of your connections is more important than the number. The Sociometer Theory reminds us that while belonging matters, your self-esteem should not rely solely on others' opinions (Leary et al., 1995).

Let this be the chapter where you decide to step down from pedestals that are not rightfully yours and start building your own. The journey might be tough, but the reward is a life lived true to your most profound truth.

Chapter 7

The Journey Through Pain

P ain is a universal experience that shows up differently for everyone—loss, betrayal, failure, rejection—and often strikes unexpectedly, disrupting our life's rhythm. While pain is unavoidable, it also acts as a catalyst for change. It pushes us to confront our truths, uncover hidden strengths, and begin a journey of self-discovery. Despite its discomfort, pain can drive growth by peeling back layers of our perceived identity and revealing who we are truly meant to become.

Pain as a Mirror

Psychologists have long studied how pain acts as a mirror, reflecting the parts of ourselves we often ignore. Carl Rogers, a pioneer in humanistic psychology, emphasized the importance of congruence—aligning one's actions with one's true self. Pain often arises when there is a disconnect between who we are and how we live (Rogers, 1961). It pushes us to confront this misalignment and ask difficult questions: What am I holding onto that no longer serves me? What do I need to let go of to move forward?

Pain also uncovers unresolved wounds and insecurities. For example, Brené Brown's research on vulnerability shows that avoiding emotional discomfort only deepens our struggles. Instead, sitting with our pain and reflecting on its source helps us process and heal (Brown, 2012).

Pain is not meant to punish us; it exists to reveal what needs attention and healing.

The Breaking Point

There comes a moment in every painful journey when we feel like we've reached our limit. This is the breaking point. The moment when the weight of pain becomes unbearable. Psychologists call this a "turning point," a crucial moment when we either fall into despair or choose to rise.

Angela Duckworth's research on grit reveals that perseverance in the face of adversity is a key predictor of success. The breaking point is often where grit is formed. It is where we choose to rise, fight, and regain our strength (Duckworth, 2016). This decision is not easy. It requires letting go of the familiar, even when it is painful, and stepping into the unknown. It is in these moments that transformation begins.

Growth Through Pain

Pain is often called a teacher, and for good reason. It pushes us to grow by forcing us to adapt, persevere, and rebuild. Research on post-traumatic growth by Richard Tedeschi and Lawrence Calhoun shows that people who face adversity often come out stronger, more resilient, and with a greater sense of purpose (Tedeschi & Calhoun, 2004).

• Clarity: Pain provides clarity by removing illusions and showing us what truly matters. It compels us to prioritize our values and align our actions with them.

• Resilience: Pain builds resilience by teaching us that we are stronger than we realize. Each time we overcome a challenge; we prove to ourselves that we can endure.

• Compassion: Pain cultivates compassion by strengthening our empathy for others. It reminds us that we are all linked through shared experiences of struggle and healing.

The Process of Transformation

Transformation through pain is a process, not a one-time event. It requires time, patience, and a willingness to put in effort.

1. Acknowledgment: The first step is to acknowledge the pain. This involves allowing yourself to feel it, to name it, and to accept it as part of your experience.

Recognizing pain is not a sign of weakness. Pain is the initial step toward healing.

2. Reflection: The second step is to consider what the pain is teaching you. What does it reveal about your values, your boundaries, or your relationships?

- For example, pain might indicate the need to establish clearer boundaries or to focus more on self-care.

3. Action: The final step is to take action. This could mean seeking therapy, journaling, or making changes in your life that align with your truth.

- Research on mindfulness-based stress reduction (MBSR) has shown that practices like meditation and journaling can help individuals process pain and reduce emotional distress (Kabat-Zinn, 1990).

The Gift of Pain

As hard as it is to endure, pain leaves behind gifts. It teaches us lessons we might not have learned otherwise. It helps us grow in ways we never imagined. It prepares us for the next chapter of our lives.

The gift of pain is not the pain itself, but what follows—clarity, strength, and resilience that grow from the journey.

Rising Through Pain

The journey through pain is one of the toughest experiences we face, but it is also one of the most transforming. Pain removes our illusions, forces us to face our truths, and guides us on a path to growth.

As you go through your own journey with pain, remember this: you are not defined by your pain. You are defined by how you rise above it. Let pain be your teacher, your guide, and your catalyst for reaching your highest potential.

Pain is not the conclusion; it is the start of something new.

Chapter 8

The Strength in Vulnerability

For much of my life, I saw vulnerability as something to avoid. I believed that being open about my struggles or feelings would only lead to judgment or disappointment. I thought that silence and self-containment signaled maturity and that showing my scars would give others ammunition. My armor became my identity. I wore it everywhere—at work, at home, even when I was alone with my thoughts.

The wounds from hurt I carried did not come from strangers. They came from those I trusted most. Pain within the walls of my own home forced me to confront the limits of my armor. I realized that no amount of self-protection could keep me from being hurt by those closest to me. The more I tried to hide my vulnerability, the more isolated and misunderstood I felt.

This was my turning point. I realized that vulnerability is not a weakness but a path to deeper connection and healing. It is not about giving others control over me but about reclaiming my own story. Vulnerability, I learned, is the courage to let yourself be seen for who you truly are—imperfect, evolving, growing, and genuine.

Vulnerability as Self-Leadership

Contrary to what I once believed, vulnerability is a form of self-leadership. It is the deliberate choice to share your truth, even when it feels risky. It is the willingness to admit you do not have all the answers, to ask for help, and to share your journey without omitting the complex parts. In leadership, vulnerability fosters trust. Teams, families, and communities grow stronger when people feel safe to speak honestly and show up as their whole selves.

I remember a time when I was leading a project that was falling apart behind the scenes. I could have pretended everything was fine, but I chose to share my concerns with my team. That moment of honesty opened the door for others to share ideas, admit their own struggles, and work together toward a solution. The project's turnaround was not just about strategy, but about the trust we built through mutual openness.

The Science Behind Vulnerability

William James's research on self-esteem shows that our sense of worth depends on how we compare our achievements to our goals (James, as cited in Snyder, Maddux, & Baron, 2012). When we set unrealistic standards or ignore our flaws, our self-worth drops. Being vulnerable breaks this cycle by helping us accept our limitations, set realistic goals, and recognize our progress.

In a research study by Wong and Yeung (2017), it showed that self-compassion—treating yourself with kindness and understanding—enables you to face vulnerability without shame. When I began practicing self-compassion, I noticed that being open about my struggles became easier. I stopped seeing setbacks as personal failures and instead viewed them as opportunities for growth.

Neely, Mohammed, and Roberts (2009) found that self-compassion, along with self-acceptance and self-esteem, boosts resilience in the face of stress. Vulnerability, then, is not just about sharing your story; it is about developing the psychological resources to recover and thrive. It is the foundation of emotional strength.

Vulnerability and Connection

One of the most important lessons vulnerability has taught me is that it is the foundation of real connection. When you allow yourself to be seen, you encourage others to do the same. Relationships grow stronger when people feel safe to share their fears, hopes, and failures without fear of ridicule or rejection.

I remember a talk I had with a close friend during a very tough time in my life. Instead of acting like I was okay, I opened up about my fears and doubts. To my surprise, she shared her own struggles too, and we both ended the conversation feeling lighter and more understood. That moment showed me that vulnerability is not a one-way thing. It is an invitation to realness from both sides.

If you've ever felt disconnected or misunderstood, think about whether you're allowing others to see the real you. Often, what we see as rejection is actually because we're hiding our true selves. When you are honest about who you are, you open the door to genuine empathy and support.

Vulnerability as a Healing Practice

Vulnerability is also crucial for healing. Many of us carry pain from the past that we try to suppress or ignore. Healing cannot happen in hiding. It requires us to confront our wounds, grieve losses, and ask for what we need. I learned this lesson after a series of personal setbacks that left me feeling lost. Only when I started sharing my story—with safe, trusted people—did I begin to find relief and perspective.

Healing through vulnerability is not about oversharing or seeking pity. It is about choosing honesty over denial. It involves allowing yourself to feel, process, and move forward intentionally. Sometimes, that means seeking professional help, joining a support group, or simply confiding in someone you trust.

Practical Ways to Embrace Vulnerability

Embracing vulnerability is a daily practice. Here are a few ways to start:

1. Name Your Feelings: Instead of dismissing discomfort, pause and recognize what you're feeling. Allow yourself to experience emotions without judgment.

2. Share Selectively: Pick one person you trust and share something intangible (like an insecurity, a hope, or a

recent challenge). Notice how it feels to be honest.

3. Ask for Help: If you're struggling, reach out. Let someone know what you need, even if all you want is a listening ear.

4. Reflect on Your Growth: Keep a journal of moments when you chose vulnerability. Over time, you will see how these choices build resilience and self-trust.

5. Model Openness: Whether at work, home, or in your community, be the person who creates space for others to be authentic. Your example will inspire others to follow.

Vulnerability and the Pedestal Philosophy

Sitting on your own pedestal means standing firm in your truth, being willing to show all of yourself, and open to learning along the way. Vulnerability strengthens your pedestal, not weakens it, because it is built on authenticity rather than illusion. When you honor your story and your growth, you motivate others to do the same.

The Pedestal Philosophy encourages living as your whole self, not just your highlight reel. Vulnerability serves as the bridge between your inner world and outer presence. It enables you to lead, love, and live with integrity.

A Personal Reflection

There was a time when I believed I had to have everything together before I could help others. I thought my influence depended on knowing all the answers. I've learned that my most meaningful impact comes from sharing my journey honestly, including my missteps and lessons along the way. When I let go of the need to appear invulnerable, I found a deeper well of strength and connection. I was able to support others not from a position of superiority but from true empathy. My relationships became more meaningful, my work more fulfilling, and my sense of self more grounded.

Your Invitation

If you're reading this and struggling with the idea of being vulnerable, know that you're not alone. It takes courage to allow yourself to be seen, to face rejection, and to accept imperfection. The benefits are real: deeper relationships, increased resilience, and a life aligned with your core values.

Begin where you are. Share a little more of yourself than you feel comfortable doing. Believe that your story matters. Remember that every act of vulnerability strengthens your foundation and brings you closer to the person you are becoming.

Vulnerability is not a flaw. It is the source of your strength, your connection, and your deepest growth. Embrace it, practice it, and watch as your life expands in meaning and potential.

Chapter 9

Relationships and the Pedestal

Relationships are some of the most beautiful and challenging parts of our lives. They can lift us up, inspire us, and change us, but they can also test the very core of who we are. They act as mirrors, showing not just how we connect with others but also how we relate to ourselves. At the heart of every relationship—whether romantic, family, or friendship—lies the question: Am I staying true to myself?

In romantic relationships, especially, it becomes easy to lose sight of who we are. Love often blurs boundaries, persuading us to compromise parts of ourselves in the name of connection or, dare I say, "in the name of love." As Brené Brown wisely said, "Authenticity is the daily practice of letting go of who we think we are supposed to be and embracing who we are" (2012).

Sitting on someone else's pedestal breeds toxicity. It causes an imbalance of power, where one person's validation becomes the other's lifeline. Over time, this dynamic can result in control, resentment, and even abuse. The pedestal turns into a trap, and the longer we stay on it, the harder it gets to step down.

The Danger

One of the most dangerous things we can do in a relationship is lose ourselves. It does not happen all at once; it is gradual and almost imperceptible. It begins with small compromises: saying yes when we want to say no, silencing our opinions to avoid conflict, or putting their happiness above our own. At first, it feels like love. Over time, these compromises erode our authenticity, leaving us increasingly disconnected from who we are and who we aspire to be. Yes, I said who we are to become. Just as on the other side of fear lies an awakening of success, so too are your dreams delayed when you're in a place where you do not belong. As Maya Angelou said, "You may not control all the events that happen to you, but you can decide not to be reduced by them" (Angelou, 2009).

Being in a relationship should never mean losing yourself. True love does not ask you to shrink, dim your light, or mold yourself into someone else's idea of perfect. You are not a puppet. It honors your individuality, your truth, and your worth. When we rely on someone else to define our value, we give them the power to shape us, and that power is often misused.

The Hard Truths

Loving is difficult. It demands vulnerability, patience, and a willingness to grow alongside someone else. Loving another person should never come at the expense of loving yourself. When we give up our self-worth for the sake of a relationship, we open ourselves up to pain, loneliness, abuse, and abandonment. As Gayle Forman wrote, "Love is not something you protect; it is something you risk" (Forman, 2009). However, this risk should never mean risking your sense of self.

Leaving is difficult. Walking away from a relationship, even if it is toxic, can feel like ripping apart a piece of your soul. It is not just losing the person—it is losing the future you imagined with them. It is fearing the start of over, being alone, and not knowing who you are without them.

Establishing boundaries is challenging. It requires saying no when you've been conditioned to say yes. It involves standing firm in your truth, even when it is uncomfortable or met with resistance. Boundaries are not walls—they are acts of self-love. As Prentis Hemphill said, "Boundaries are the distance at which I can love you and me simultaneously" (Hemphill, 2020). They safeguard your peace, energy, and sense of self. However, setting them demands courage, especially in relationships where boundaries have never been established.

Recovering is difficult. Healing from a toxic relationship is one of the toughest challenges you will face (trust me, I've been there). It is not just about healing the pain—it is about rediscovering who you are. And if you never truly knew yourself, it becomes even harder. It involves accepting your role in enabling, admitting your toxicity, and unlearning the patterns that led you to be put on someone else's pedestal in the first place.

The recovery process is messy. Some days, you will feel strong and empowered. Other days, you will question whether you made the right choice. You will grieve the relationship, even if it was not healthy, because love—no matter how flawed—leaves a mark. As Bell Hooks wrote, "Love is an act of will—namely, both an intention and an action" (hooks, 2000). And sometimes, stepping off the pedestal is the bravest act of love you can give yourself.

Building

The key to healthy relationships is building your own pedestal and remaining firmly grounded in it. This does not mean excluding others or refusing to compromise. It involves knowing your worth and refusing to allow anyone else to define it. It means loving yourself so deeply that your happiness is not dependent on someone else's approval.

When you build your own pedestal, you lay a foundation of self-worth that no one can shake. You establish boundaries that protect your peace, communicate your needs confidently, and choose partners who uplift and support you rather than diminish you.

Healthy relationships are not about perfection; they are about balance. As Esther Perel reminds us, "The quality of our relationships determines the quality of our lives" (Perel, 2017). They are about two individuals standing on their own pedestals, supporting each other without losing themselves. They are built on mutual respect, trust, and a shared commitment to growth.

The Power of Authentic Love

Authentic love is transformative. It does not ask you to change; it inspires growth. It does not demand perfection; it accepts your flaws. It does not put you on a pedestal; it stands beside you, hand in hand, as equals.

When you love genuinely, you build a relationship grounded in truth, not illusion. You respect each other's individuality while creating a life together. You communicate honestly, set boundaries kindly, and face challenges with compassion and understanding.

But most importantly, authentic love begins with you. It starts with your relationship with yourself—how you see, treat, and value yourself. As Rupi Kaur beautifully expressed, "How you love yourself is how you teach others to love you" (Kaur, 2017). When you love yourself first, you set the standard for how others should love you. You become the author of your own story, not a character in someone else's narrative.

Relationships are challenging, but they are worth it when built on authenticity and self-worth. The greatest act of love you can do is stay true to who you are, regardless of the relationship.

Because when you climb onto someone else's pedestal, you lose your power. And when you step down, you take it back.

When you choose to share your life with someone, make sure they are standing on their own pedestal, too, because true love is not about losing yourself. It is about finding someone who inspires you to be more of who you already are.

Chapter 10

The Courage to Define and Stand in Your Truth

S tanding in your truth and defining it is one of the bravest acts of self-love and empowerment you can do. It demands confronting others' expectations, quieting your inner critic, and accepting who you truly are. But perhaps the most powerful part of this journey is realizing that reclaiming your power starts with reclaiming your truth.

The idea of truth is deeply personal. It is not about fitting into societal norms or meeting outside expectations. It is about aligning with your values, beliefs, and purpose. As Brené Brown (2012) explains, "Authenticity is the daily practice of letting go of who we think we're supposed to be and embracing who we are." This practice, however, is not without its challenges. It requires vulnerability, resilience, and the courage to stand firm even when the world tries to shake you.

Reclaiming your truth means taking ownership of your story. It involves no longer letting others define who you are, what you're capable of, or what you deserve. For many, this process starts with unlearning. We need to unlearn the stories we've been told about ourselves and replace them with the truths we hold deep in our hearts.

As Bell Hooks (2000) reminds us, "Knowing how to be solitary is central to the art of loving. When we can be alone, we can be with others without using them as a means of escape." This solitude is vital for self-reflection. It helps us discover the layers of conditioning, fear, and doubt that have prevented us from living authentically. Only then can we reclaim the power we've unconsciously surrendered.

Standing in your truth takes bravery, not the absence of fear, but the willingness to act despite it. It is about speaking up when staying silent feels easier, setting boundaries when complying seems more comfortable, and choosing yourself even if it feels selfish. As Maya Angelou (2009) so eloquently stated, "Courage is the most important of all the virtues because without courage, you cannot practice any other virtue consistently."

But courage does not mean you will not face resistance. In fact, standing in your truth often invites criticism, rejection, and misunderstanding. People may question your choices or try to silence your voice, but that's where your power resides. It is in your ability to stay steadfast. Esther Perel (2017) emphasizes how important resilience is, noting that "Authenticity is not about being brutally honest; it is about being true to yourself in a way that fosters connection rather than alienation."

Reclaiming Your Power

Reclaiming your power is an act of self-liberation. It involves recognizing that your worth is inherent and that no one else has the right to determine your value. This journey begins with self-awareness—understanding your needs, desires, and boundaries—and continues with self-advocacy.

As Rupi Kaur (2017) wrote, "You do not just wake up and become the butterfly. Growth is a process." Reclaiming your power is not an instant change; it is a journey of growth, healing, and self-discovery. It requires you to let go of the need for external validation and trust that your truth is enough.

One of the most powerful tools in this process is boundary-setting. Boundaries are not about shutting people out; they are about creating space for yourself. Prentis Hemphill (2020) describes boundaries as "the distance at which I can love you and me simultaneously." They protect your peace, honor your truth, and ensure that your energy is directed toward what truly matters.

When you define and stand in your truth, you not only reclaim your power but also encourage others to do the same. Authenticity is contagious. It creates a ripple effect, inspiring those around you to embrace their own truths and live more intentionally.

Living authentically does not mean you will not face challenges. It means you will confront them with clarity, confidence, and purpose. As Gayle Forman (2009) wrote, "Sometimes you make choices in life, and sometimes choices make you." By choosing to stand in your truth, you take responsibility for your life and create a future that reflects who you are.

Having the courage to define and stand in your truth is the foundation of personal empowerment. It involves reclaiming your story, setting boundaries, and living genuinely. Although the journey might be tough, the rewards are priceless. You will gain a deeper understanding of yourself, feel more connected to your purpose, and tap into the unshakable power that comes from living in alignment with your truth.

Chapter 11

Reclaiming Your Power

Then are moments in life when you realize your power
has faded, sometimes quietly and sometimes suddenly. It
occurs in subtle ways. When you silence your own voice, let
others' needs take precedence, or find yourself living by rules you
never established. Reclaiming your power is a deliberate act of
returning to yourself. It involves gathering the scattered pieces of
your agency, confidence, and self-trust, and declaring that your life
belongs to you.

This is the core of the Pedestal Philosophy. Essentially, it
emphasizes that your worth is not determined by others' standards
or expectations. It involves stepping down from the pedestals
others have placed you on and intentionally building your own—a
space where your needs, values, and dreams are respected without
apology. When you reclaim your power, you're not waiting for
someone else to lift you up. Instead, you're choosing to stand tall

on your own pedestal, knowing you're worthy of being seen, heard, and valued by yourself first.

This journey starts with awareness. Many people go through their days on autopilot, influenced by routines, obligations, and others' expectations. It is easy to forget that you have choices, that your voice matters, and that you can change direction whenever you want. Reclaiming your power begins with noticing where you have given it away. Sometimes it is in relationships where your boundaries are crossed, at work where your efforts are ignored, or in the stories you carry from childhood. The first step is to pause and ask: Where am I living by someone else's script? Where do I feel small, silent, or invisible?

Psychological theory offers a helpful perspective for understanding this process. Self-determination theory highlights that autonomy—the capacity to make choices aligned with your true self—is a fundamental psychological need (Deci & Ryan, 2000). When autonomy is restricted, motivation, well-being, and even creativity decline. Reclaiming your power involves restoring autonomy in your life. This could mean speaking up in a meeting, declining a request that drains you, or finally pursuing a dream you've deferred. Every act of self-direction, no matter how small, is a form of reclamation.

Reclaiming power also involves facing the beliefs and habits that have kept you playing small. Many of these beliefs are passed down from family, culture, or past experiences. You may have learned that it is safer to stay quiet, that wanting more is selfish, or that mistakes determine your worth. These internalized messages can be persistent, but they are not permanent. Through reflection and sometimes with the support of a therapist or coach, you can challenge and rewrite these beliefs. Asking questions like "Whose voice is this?" or "Does this belief serve me?" opens the door to new possibilities.

Self-compassion is a powerful ally in this process. According to Neff (2003), self-compassion means responding to your own struggles with kindness instead of harsh judgment. When you start to reclaim your power, it is natural to feel guilt, fear, or regret about past decisions. Self-compassion helps you move forward without being burdened by self-criticism. It encourages you to see your efforts as brave, not selfish, and to treat yourself with the same understanding you would give a close friend.

Reclaiming your power also involves making peace with imperfection. The pursuit of perfection is a common trap that keeps many people stuck. You may hesitate to take action until you feel confident, prepared, or "good enough." In reality, waiting for perfect conditions is another way of giving your power to fear. Growth happens when you act despite uncertainty, trusting that you can handle whatever comes. The sociometer theory (Leary et al., 1995) reminds us that our sense of self-esteem is shaped by social feedback; however, true power lies in learning to validate yourself, regardless of external opinions.

Boundaries are vital tools for reclaiming power. Setting boundaries is not about pushing others away but about safeguarding your energy and values. It is a way of saying, "This is what I need to stay well," and honoring that need without apology. Boundaries can be as simple as carving out time to rest, turning down a social invitation, or communicating your limits at work. Every time you set a boundary; you affirm your right to live on your own terms.

The process of reclaiming power is ongoing. It is not a one-time declaration, but a series of choices made every day. There will be setbacks and times when old habits resurface. The key is persistence. Celebrate your progress, no matter how small. Notice how your sense of self changes when you consistently choose yourself. Over time, you will find that your life feels more authentic, vibrant, and aligned with your deepest values.

Reclaiming your power does not mean rejecting connection or community. In fact, empowered people tend to be more generous, compassionate, and open. When you're grounded in your own strength, you can support others without losing yourself. You can participate in relationships, work, and service from a place of abundance rather than obligation.

Ultimately, reclaiming your power is about returning to the truth that you are the creator of your own life. You have the right and responsibility to shape your story, pursue what matters, and honor your needs. The Pedestal Philosophy reminds you that your power belongs to you, and your life is yours to direct. The world may present many distractions and demands, but your power is always waiting to be reclaimed. It exists in every choice, boundary, and act of self-respect.

Take a moment to reflect on where you've given your power away and commit to reclaiming it. Remember, regaining your power is not selfish; it is essential for a life filled with purpose, fulfillment, and joy.

Chapter 12

Building Your Pedestal

There is a deep difference between knowing you deserve better and actually building the foundation that supports your best self. Building your own pedestal is not about waiting for someone else to recognize your worth or give you a platform. It is about intentionally creating a base that can hold you steady through every season of your life—a base you design, strengthen, and maintain with purpose.

Many people spend years craving external validation, hoping that someone will finally notice them, acknowledge their efforts, and give them permission to shine. Nevertheless, the truth is, waiting for someone else's approval is a never-ending game. The only pedestal strong enough to support your growth is the one you create for yourself.

The Blueprint: Self-Awareness

Building your pedestal starts with self-awareness. Before you can create anything durable, you need to understand what you're standing on. This involves honestly examining your values, passions, and beliefs. What truly matters to you? What makes you feel alive? What are your non-negotiables—the lines you will not cross, regardless of the pressure?

Writing in a journal, practicing meditation, or recording voice notes can all help you clarify your answers. The point is not to come up with a list that impresses others, but to figure out what's truly real for you. This is your personal roadmap. If your foundation is built on someone else's expectations or the latest trends, it will not last. But if it is grounded in your own truth, it will stand strong against any challenges.

Clearing the Ground: Letting Go of Old Narratives

Before you can build, you need to clear away what no longer serves you. Many of us carry limiting beliefs from childhood, culture, or past relationships—stories that tell us we are "too much," "not enough," or unworthy of happiness. These beliefs are like debris that weaken your foundation.

Take time to recognize and question these internalized messages. Where did they originate? Are they accurate, or were they passed down? Replace them with affirmations that mirror your current reality and potential. This process is not about denying your past but about making space for your future.

Laying the First Stones: Autonomy and Ownership

Self-Determination Theory, developed by Edward Deci and Richard Ryan, emphasizes autonomy as a key need for personal growth and fulfillment (Deci & Ryan, 1985). Autonomy is the freedom to make choices that align with your true desires, not just what others expect. Building your pedestal means taking ownership of your decisions, both big and small.

Begin by making one decision each day that is solely for yourself. It could be as simple as choosing what to eat, how to spend your free time, or which project to take on. Every act of independence lays a brick in your foundation. Over time, these choices accumulate, strengthening your sense of control and self-confidence.

Competence: Building Confidence Brick by Brick

As you gain autonomy, focus on competence—the sense of mastery and accomplishment that comes from setting and achieving meaningful goals. William James's self-esteem formula reminds us that confidence grows when our successes are aligned with our own aspirations, not with what others expect (James, 1890).

Set goals that truly matter to you, not just those that seem impressive on paper. Break them into small, manageable steps, and recognize every milestone. Each achievement, no matter how small, is a building block of your confidence. Over time, your self-assurance will grow—not from perfection, but from persistence.

Reinforcing with Relatedness: Meaningful Connections

No pedestal is built in isolation. Relatedness, another pillar of Self-Determination Theory, involves forming connections that support your growth and well-being. Seek out people who encourage you to be your best self, challenge you to grow, and celebrate your victories without jealousy or resentment.

Building your pedestal might mean letting go of relationships that drain you or force you to shrink. This can be hard, especially if those relationships are old. Remember, you're not abandoning others; you're focusing on your own health and happiness. The right people will respect your boundaries and support you.

Boundaries: The Protective Barrier

Boundaries are the protective walls around your pedestal. They define what is acceptable and what is not, what you will allow into your life and what you will keep out. Setting boundaries is not about shutting people out, but about honoring your needs and safeguarding your energy.

Begin by pinpointing areas where you're feeling resentment, exhaustion, or overwhelm. These are often signs that you need to set or reinforce a boundary. Work on saying no without feeling guilty and yes without feeling like you owe someone. Clearly and consistently communicate your boundaries. As time goes on, you will find it easier to stand your ground, and others will start to respect your limits.

Self-Compassion: The Mortar that Holds It Together

No foundation is perfect. There will be cracks, setbacks, and moments of doubt. Kristin Neff's Self-Compassion Theory teaches us that treating ourselves with kindness and understanding, especially during difficult times, is essential for resilience and growth (Neff, 2003).

When you make a mistake or fall short of your standards, resist the urge to criticize or punish yourself. Instead, offer yourself the same grace you would give a friend. Use setbacks as opportunities to learn and reinforce your foundation. Self-compassion is the mortar that holds your pedestal together, filling in the gaps and keeping it strong.

Designing Your Environment

Your physical and social environment greatly influences your foundation. Keep reminders of your values and goals nearby—such as vision boards, quotes, or objects that motivate you. Establish routines and rituals that strengthen your commitment to yourself, like morning meditation, weekly check-ins, or monthly progress reviews.

If possible, create an environment that minimizes distractions and temptations that lead you away from your goal. This could mean limiting time spent with negative influences, curating your social media feeds, or organizing your space to support your habits and routines.

Celebrating Progress and Maintenance

Building your own pedestal is not a one-time event, but an ongoing process. Make it a habit to celebrate your progress, no matter how small. Recognize the courage it takes to choose yourself, set boundaries, pursue your goals, and stand tall in your truth.

Regularly inspect your foundation for cracks or weaknesses. Are there beliefs, habits, or relationships that need to be released or reinforced? Are you honoring your needs and values, or have you strayed from your path? Use these check-ins as chances to realign and recommit to your growth.

Letting Go of What No Longer Serves

As your confidence grows stronger, you may find that certain commitments, habits, or relationships no longer fit. Letting go can be difficult, but it is necessary for continued growth. Trust that by releasing what no longer benefits you, you make space for new opportunities and connections that match your evolving self.

This process mirrors Maslow's idea of self-actualization—the ongoing journey of realizing your potential and accepting change (Maslow, 1943). Growth requires courage, adaptability, and a willingness to face the unknown. Each time you release what is not meant for you, you strengthen your foundation and get closer to the life you want.

Community: Building Together

While your pedestal is deeply personal, it does not have to be solitary. Find community—friends, mentors, or groups—who support your journey and share your values. Community offers encouragement, accountability, and inspiration. Share your story, celebrate others' successes, and give support when needed. By building your pedestal, you encourage others to do the same.

Practical Blueprint for Building Your Pedestal

1. Clarify Your Values: Write down what matters most to you. Use these values as a guide for your decisions and boundaries.

2. Set meaningful goals: Select goals that align with your true desires. Break them into actionable steps and monitor your progress.

3. Establish boundaries: Recognize where you feel drained and set limits to safeguard your energy and well-being.

4. Practice Self-Compassion: Treat yourself with kindness when you stumble. Learn from setbacks and keep building.

5. Curate Your Environment: Arrange your space and routines to foster your growth and reduce distractions.

6. Celebrate Wins: Consistently recognize your accomplishments and progress.

7. Revisit and Adjust: Regularly evaluate your foundation and make updates as you grow.

Living from Your Pedestal

Building your own pedestal is a bold act of self-respect and self-leadership. It declares that your life, happiness, and fulfillment are worth investing in. When you stand on your pedestal, you feel a sense of integrity. Your actions, words, and values align. You become more resilient when facing challenges, more confident in your decisions, and more compassionate toward yourself and others.

Most importantly, you no longer wait for someone else to recognize your worth or give you permission to shine. You become the architect of your own story, the builder of your own foundation. Your pedestal is not a place of isolation but a platform for connection, growth, and contribution.

Let this chapter serve as your blueprint. With each brick you lay—each act of self-leadership, compassion, and courage—you strengthen your foundation. Honor your journey. Build your pedestal with purpose and pride, and stand on it every day, knowing you are worthy of the life you create.

Chapter 13
Climbing on Your Pedestal

There comes a moment in every journey of self-discovery when you must choose to do more than just lay a foundation for your worth—you must be willing to stand on it, fully visible and unapologetic. This is the core of climbing onto your pedestal. It is a deliberate, brave act, a statement that you are ready to claim your space in the world, not as a copy of someone else, but as the most authentic expression of yourself.

Many people spend years, sometimes decades, quietly working on themselves. They read, reflect, heal, and grow. They learn to set boundaries, define their values, and nurture self-love. But there's a difference between quietly knowing your worth and boldly living it out loud. Stepping onto your pedestal is the moment when all the internal work turns into external action. It is when you stop hiding in the shadows of doubt or fear and step into the light, ready to be seen for who you truly are.

This act is not about arrogance or seeking attention. It is about presence. It is about showing up for yourself and for the world in a way that honors your journey, your struggles, and your triumphs. Climbing onto your pedestal is a commitment to visibility, to using your voice, and to allowing yourself to be celebrated for your uniqueness. It is about taking up space with intention and purpose.

The fear of being seen is real. For many, the idea of stepping up and standing out feels intimidating. Memories of past criticism, rejection, or failure can haunt you, whispering that it is safer to stay small. Society often teaches us that humility means shrinking ourselves, that confidence is arrogance, and that standing out is risky. But the truth is, you cannot inspire, lead, or fully live from the sidelines. The world needs your light, your voice, and your presence.

Climbing onto your pedestal begins with a decision. It is the decision to stop waiting for perfect timing, more confidence, or someone else's permission. It is the decision to trust that you are ready, even if you do not feel fully prepared. This leap is rarely comfortable. In fact, it often brings a surge of doubt and vulnerability. But discomfort is not a sign that you're on the wrong path—it is a sign that you're growing.

One of the first challenges when climbing onto your pedestal is facing the fear of judgment. The moment you step into the spotlight, you become visible not only to supporters but also to critics. People might project their insecurities, misunderstand your intentions, or question your choices. This is unavoidable. What's important is not the lack of criticism, but your ability to stay true to your values and intentions despite it.

Here, the idea of psychological resilience is important. Resilience is the ability to recover from setbacks, adjust to challenges, and keep working toward your goals despite obstacles. Research shows that resilient people are more likely to keep going in the face of difficulty, seeing setbacks as chances to grow rather than reasons to give up (Masten, 2001). When you stand tall on your pedestal, resilience becomes your supporter. It helps you withstand the storms of external opinion and stay true to your own truth.

Another key ingredient is self-compassion. Climbing onto your pedestal does not mean you will never make mistakes or doubt yourself. It means you are willing to show up anyway, to be imperfect and still deserve your own respect. Kristin Neff's self-compassion theory reminds us that treating ourselves with kindness and understanding, especially during vulnerable moments, is vital for ongoing growth and courage (Neff, 2003). When you stumble or falter, self-compassion helps you recover, learn, and keep climbing.

Visibility also carries responsibility. When you stand tall, others will see you as an example, whether consciously or unconsciously. This does not mean you need to be perfect or have all the answers. Instead, it is an invitation to lead with integrity, to demonstrate authenticity, and to motivate others to do the same. Your willingness to be seen, with all your strengths and flaws, encourages others to step onto their own pedestals. This is how transformation spreads—not through perfection, but through courage and honesty.

Climbing onto your pedestal often means revisiting old stories about worthiness and belonging. Many of us carry narratives from childhood, culture, or past experiences that tell us we are too much, not enough, or unworthy of celebration. These stories can be powerful, but they are not the truth of who you are. Part of the climb is learning to recognize and rewrite these stories. It is about replacing limiting beliefs with affirmations of your value and potential.

One practical step is to establish rituals that reinforce your commitment to standing tall. This could include daily affirmations, visualization exercises, or journaling about your intentions and progress. You might create a physical space in your home that reminds you of your worth—a corner filled with objects, quotes, or images that inspire you. These rituals act as anchors, helping you return to your pedestal when life tries to pull you down.

Another important aspect is seeking and accepting support. Climbing on your pedestal does not mean doing it alone. Surround yourself with people who celebrate your growth, encourage you to shine, and remind you of your strengths when you forget. Community can be a powerful source of encouragement and accountability. At the same time, be discerning about whose feedback you allow to influence you. Not everyone will understand your journey, and that is okay.

As you keep climbing, you may reach new heights and face new challenges. Each level of visibility offers its own lessons. You might find yourself exploring new opportunities, responsibilities, or relationships. The pedestal is not a fixed spot—it is a dynamic platform that changes as you do. You may need to adjust your stance, strengthen your foundation, or take breaks to rest and think. The main point is to keep climbing, stay committed to visibility, and continue honoring your growth.

It is also important to celebrate your progress. Too often, we focus on how far we still have to go and forget to acknowledge how far we have already come. Take time to recognize your achievements, both big and small. Celebrate the moments when you spoke your truth, set a boundary, or pursued a dream. These victories show your courage and commitment.

Climbing on your pedestal is not about reaching a final goal. It is about embracing the process of becoming. It is about showing up for yourself every day with honesty, courage, and self-respect. It is about being willing to be seen, not as a perfect icon, but as a real, breathing person with a story worth sharing.

The rewards of standing on your pedestal are significant. You feel a deeper sense of fulfillment, knowing you are living in line with your values. You build greater confidence, resilience, and self-trust. You motivate others to do the same, creating a ripple effect of empowerment and authenticity. Most importantly, you find the freedom that comes from living as your true self.

If you are standing at the base of your pedestal, wondering if you're ready to climb, know that you are not alone. Every person who has chosen to live authentically has faced the same doubts and fears. The difference is not in the absence of fear, but in the willingness to act despite it. Take the first step, even if it is small. Speak your truth, share your story, or pursue a goal that matters to you. Each step you take builds your confidence and strengthens your foundation.

Remember that you are worthy of being seen. Your voice matters. Your presence makes a difference. The world does not need another imitation — it needs your unique light. Climbing onto your pedestal is a gift to yourself and everyone inspired by your courage.

As you move forward on your journey, keep returning to your pedestal. When life becomes tough, when criticism hurts, or when doubt appears, remind yourself of the work you've done to build your foundation. Reconnect with your values, your purpose, and your vision. Trust that you are exactly where you need to be, and that every step you take proves your strength.

Let this chapter be your invitation to climb. Not just once, but every day. To choose visibility over hiding, courage over comfort, and self-respect over self-doubt. The pedestal is yours to claim, and the view from the top is more beautiful than you can imagine. Not because it is perfect, but because it is real.

Climbing on your pedestal is not an act of pride, but an act of love. It celebrates your journey, declares your worth, and commits to living fully. May you climb bravely, stand tall, and shine brightly, knowing that you are enough just as you are.

Chapter 14

Setbacks and Rebuilding

When Your Pedestal Cracks

N o matter how carefully you build your pedestal, life will eventually test its strength. Even the most intentional foundations are susceptible to the unexpected—loss, failure, heartbreak, disappointment, or the gradual erosion of self-doubt. The truth is no one is immune to setbacks. What separates those who thrive from those who stay stuck is not the absence of cracks but the willingness to notice, repair, and rebuild.

The myth of the unbreakable pedestal is alluring. We want to believe that once we've done the hard work of building our self-worth, setting boundaries, and standing in our truth, we'll be protected from future pain. But life is always changing, not fixed. Change, challenge, and uncertainty are unavoidable. Sometimes, the cracks appear suddenly—a job loss, a betrayal, or harsh criticism that hits too close to home. Other times, they develop quietly and gradually, as old habits come back, or we drift away from our values.

When your pedestal cracks, it can feel like failure. You might question your progress, doubt your strength, or feel ashamed that you are struggling again. But cracks are not proof that you are broken or unworthy. They are evidence that you are alive, growing, and engaged in the messy, beautiful work of being human.

Recognizing the Cracks

The first step in rebuilding is recognizing when your pedestal is no longer supporting you properly. This requires honesty and self-awareness. Cracks might show up as exhaustion, resentment, anxiety, or a feeling of disconnection from oneself. You might notice you're saying yes when you want to say no, tolerating disrespect, or losing sight of your own needs.

Instead of ignoring these warning signs, pause and pay attention. Ask yourself: What feels off right now? Where am I compromising my values or boundaries? What am I avoiding, and why? Self-reflection is not about blame, but about gaining a deeper understanding. It takes courage to admit that something needs attention.

The Emotional Impact of Setbacks

Setbacks often bring a mix of tough emotions—frustration, sadness, anger, and sometimes shame. It is common to feel like you're back at square one, especially after working hard to build your confidence and resilience. However, setbacks do not erase your progress. Instead, they serve as opportunities to deepen your self-understanding and recommit to yourself.

Allow yourself to feel whatever arises. Suppressing or minimizing your emotions only worsens the cracks. Instead, practice self-compassion. Remind yourself that everyone experiences setbacks and that your worth is not diminished by struggles. Kristin Neff's research on self-compassion shows that treating yourself kindly during tough times fosters greater resilience and well-being (Neff, 2003). Talk to yourself like you would a close friend—gently, supportively, and without judgment.

Learning from the Cracks

Every setback holds a lesson. Sometimes, cracks appear because we've neglected our needs for too long, stretched ourselves too thin, or fallen back into old habits. Other times, they happen because of circumstances beyond our control. Either way, each crack is a chance to learn more about yourself and what you need to thrive.

Ask yourself: What led to this setback? Was it a boundary I ignored, a value I sacrificed, or a relationship that became exhausting? What can I do differently next time? Reflection is not about perfection but about growth. Be honest, but also gentle. The aim is not to prevent all future issues but to get better at noticing and fixing them early.

Rebuilding with Intention

Once you identify where your pedestal needs repair, it is time to rebuild. Start small by focusing on one area—a boundary to strengthen, a value to realign with, or a self-care practice to prioritize. While the temptation may be to overhaul everything at once, sustainable change occurs gradually.

Rebuilding also involves asking for help when needed. We often think we have to fix everything on our own, but support is essential for resilience. Reach out to trusted friends, mentors, or professionals. Share your struggles honestly and let yourself receive encouragement, perspective, or practical advice. Community is not just for celebrations; it is for rebuilding too.

Rituals of Renewal

Rituals can serve as powerful tools for healing and renewal. This might involve a simple daily check-in with yourself, a regular journaling habit, or a symbolic act like writing down what you want to release and burning the paper. Rituals mark the shift from breakdown to rebuilding and clearly express your intention to move forward.

Consider creating a "rebuilding ritual" for yourself. This could involve revisiting your values, updating your goals, or even physically cleaning your space as a way of making room for new growth. These acts, though small, reinforce your commitment to yourself and help you shift from self-criticism to self-empowerment.

Embracing Flexibility and Adaptation

Flexibility is one of the key qualities in the rebuilding process. Being too rigid can make things worse by holding onto what's no longer working. Instead, be open to adapting. Rebuilding might mean letting go of old dreams, relationships, or identities that are not serving you anymore. It could also mean redefining what success means to you, adjusting your boundaries, or finding new ways to meet your needs.

Psychologist Carol Dweck's research on the "growth mindset" shows that those who see setbacks as chances to learn and grow are more likely to succeed over time (Dweck, 2006). Adopt the idea that you are always changing, and that change is a sign of growth, not failure.

Celebrating the Strength in Rebuilding

Rebuilding is incredibly powerful. It takes courage to acknowledge when something is not working and start fresh. Every time you repair your footing, you build your resilience and strengthen your self-trust. You show yourself that you can overcome challenges and come out even stronger.

Celebrate your progress, no matter how small. Recognize the effort involved in noticing, fixing, and rebuilding. Over time, you will see that the cracks become part of your story — not as signs of weakness, but as evidence of your ability to persevere.

Moving Forward with Wisdom

Setbacks are not detours from your journey; they are part of the path. Every time your pedestal cracks and you rebuild, you gain wisdom, compassion, and a deeper understanding of yourself. The foundation you build through this process is not only stronger but also more adaptable and responsive to life's realities.

As you progress, keep in mind that perfection is not the goal. Instead, focus on staying engaged with your growth, responding to challenges with self-compassion and adaptability, and honoring your evolving needs. Your pedestal might crack, but it will not break apart if you are willing to repair and rebuild.

Let this chapter remind you that setbacks are not the end of your story. They are opportunities to renew your commitment to yourself, learn, and grow. When your world crumbles, you do not lose your worth—you discover your strength all over again. Gather the pieces, rebuild with purpose, and remember that every act of repair is an act of self-love.

Chapter 15

Controlling Your Balance

S triking a balance in life is one of the most challenging
goals. It is not something you achieve and then stop
working on; it is an ongoing process of adjustment, reflection,
and decision-making. With the constant pressure to hustle,
stay connected, and push for success, finding balance can feel
like an impossible task. However, achieving and maintaining
balance is crucial for a life filled with fulfillment, well-being, and
authenticity. It is the foundation for building a life that's not only
successful by the world's standards but also truly fulfilling on a
personal level.

Striking a balance often starts with feeling overwhelmed. You've
got responsibilities piling up—work, family, friends, self-care,
community involvement—and the pressure to excel in every area
can be overwhelming. Many people feel like they are juggling a
dozen plates, afraid that if they focus on one, the others will fall

apart. This anxiety is not unfounded; the demands of modern life are real. However, the idea that balance means dividing your time and energy equally is a myth. True balance is about making conscious choices and being willing to adjust as your needs and circumstances change.

The Pedestal Philosophy provides a unique perspective on balance. At its core, it emphasizes valuing your own worth and needs without apology. It involves placing yourself on your own pedestal—not to put yourself above others, but to acknowledge that your well-being matters. When you view balance through this lens, you're more likely to make choices aligned with your values rather than simply reacting to external pressures. You learn to say yes to what nourishes you and no to what drains you, knowing that your life is yours to shape.

Research in psychology highlights the crucial role of balance in maintaining mental health and overall well-being. According to self-determination theory, developed by Deci and Ryan (2000), people have three fundamental psychological needs: autonomy, competence, and relatedness. When these needs are met, individuals tend to be more motivated, experience better well-being, and have a more satisfying life. To maintain balance, it is essential to create space for autonomy—making choices that reflect your authentic self. This also involves developing competence through activities that challenge and fulfill you, and building meaningful connections with others to foster relatedness.

However, achieving balance does not happen by chance. It takes intentional effort and self-awareness. The first step is to pinpoint your real priorities. It is easy to get caught up in urgent tasks, but not all of them are crucial. Take the time to think about what truly matters to you. What are your core values? What brings you joy, peace, or a sense of purpose? When you're clear on your priorities, you can spend your time and energy in ways that align with your deepest goals.

Cognitive-behavioral theory offers practical strategies for staying balanced. One key principle emphasizes how thought patterns influence behavior and emotions (Beck, 2011). When you feel out of sync, pause, and examine the thoughts behind your actions. Are you acting out of fear, guilt, or a desire to please others? Are you telling yourself that you "should" do things that do not serve you? By challenging unhelpful thoughts and replacing them with more balanced views, you can make choices that promote your well-being.

Another essential aspect of controlling your balance is learning to set boundaries. Boundaries are not walls; they are guidelines that protect your time, energy, and emotional health. Setting boundaries can be uncomfortable, especially if you are used to putting others first. However, boundaries are a form of self-respect. They communicate to yourself and others that your needs are valid. The Pedestal Philosophy reminds us that standing on our own pedestal means taking responsibility for our own happiness and refusing to let guilt dictate our decisions.

Balance also needs flexibility. Life is unpredictable, and conditions can change instantly. What worked last month might not work today. Flexibility involves being open to adjusting your plans, releasing rigid expectations, and facing new challenges with creativity and resilience. This adaptability is a key sign of psychological health. According to Lazarus and Folkman's (1984) stress and coping theory, people who use adaptive coping strategies—such as problem-solving, seeking support, and reframing challenges—are better able to maintain balance and succeed amid adversity.

Self-compassion is an essential tool for maintaining balance. When you inevitably lose your balance, it is easy to fall into self-criticism or shame. Neff (2003) defines self-compassion as treating yourself with kindness and understanding during difficult moments or when you perceive failure. Instead of criticizing yourself for not doing enough, self-compassion helps you recognize your limits, forgive yourself, and start over. This gentle approach provides the psychological safety needed to try new things, make mistakes, and grow.

Controlling your balance also requires cultivating presence. The constant pressure to multitask can tempt you to divide your attention among many tasks and obligations. However, research shows that multitasking decreases productivity and raises stress (Rosen, Lim, Carrier, & Cheever, 2011). Mindfulness—the practice of giving your full attention to the present moment—can help you stay grounded. When you are present, you are more aware of when you're drifting out of balance and can make conscious adjustments.

It is important to realize that balance varies for each person and can change over time. What feels balanced in one season of life might seem restrictive or overwhelming in another. The Pedestal Philosophy promotes continual self-reflection and adaptation. Putting yourself on your own pedestal is not a one-time act but a lifelong commitment to honoring your needs and values. It involves regularly checking in with yourself and allowing yourself to grow.

Social support is another key pillar of balance. Humans are social beings, and meaningful relationships are vital for well-being. The need for relatedness, as explained by self-determination theory, is fulfilled when we feel connected, understood, and supported by others (Deci & Ryan, 2000). Build relationships that uplift you and seek support when necessary. Do not be afraid to ask for help, delegate tasks, or share your struggles. Vulnerability is not a weakness but a strength that strengthens connection and resilience.

Practical strategies can help you stay balanced in everyday life. Consider creating routines that support your physical and emotional health, such as regular exercise, healthy meals, and enough sleep. Set aside time for activities that refresh you, whether it is reading, creative hobbies, or just spending time in nature. Use tools like calendars, to-do lists, or digital reminders to stay organized and prevent feeling overwhelmed.

It is also helpful to practice saying no. Every yes is a commitment of time and energy, and saying yes to everything is a sure path to imbalance. Give yourself permission to decline requests that are not aligned with your priorities or values. Remember, every time you say no to something that does not serve you, you are saying yes to yourself.

As you continue refining your balance, take a moment to celebrate your progress. Notice when you feel centered, energized, or at peace. Acknowledge the choices you've made to honor yourself, even if they are small. The Pedestal Philosophy teaches that your life is yours to shape, and balance reflects your commitment to your well-being.

Finally, understand that controlling your balance is not about reaching perfection, but about developing awareness, flexibility, and self-respect. Some days you will feel unsteady, and that's okay. What matters most is your willingness to reconnect with yourself, make adjustments when needed, and keep moving forward. Viewing balance as a continuous practice allows you the freedom to live fully and genuinely.

Ultimately, maintaining your balance is a powerful act of self-care and self-leadership. It forms the foundation for building a life that is not only productive but also joyful and meaningful. By adopting the Pedestal Philosophy, you remind yourself that you deserve a life that feels balanced and whole. Stand confidently on your own pedestal, honor your needs, and let balance be the gift you give yourself every day.

Chapter 16

The Ripple Effect of Empowerment

E mpowerment is often seen as a deeply personal journey. You are discovering your voice, reclaiming your agency, and stepping into your own light. But from the perspective of the Pedestal Philosophy, empowerment becomes more than just an individual act; it acts as a catalyst for collective change. This philosophy teaches that real power starts when you decide to place yourself on your own pedestal—affirming your worth, honoring your story, and living in line with your values. However, the most powerful part of this philosophy is not just how it transforms you, but how it sends out ripples that influence others.

To fully grasp the concept of empowerment, it is important to recognize that it is not a static state but a dynamic process continually shaped by our beliefs, relationships, environments.

It involves a shift from feeling powerless or dependent to recognizing one's capacity to make choices, take action, and influence outcomes. This process is beautifully captured by self-determination theory, which posits that all humans have innate psychological needs for autonomy, competence, and relatedness (Deci & Ryan, 2000). When you honor these needs by claiming your pedestal, you nurture your own growth and well-being. But the Pedestal Philosophy insists that this act is not the end of the story. Instead, it is the beginning of a ripple effect that expands far beyond your own life.

The first ripple occurs within. As you embrace your worth and step onto your pedestal, your internal dialogue shifts. You begin to set healthier boundaries, pursue meaningful goals, and treat yourself with compassion. This self-acceptance is not just healing; it is contagious. When others witness your transformation, they are inspired to question their own limiting beliefs and consider what it would look like to honor themselves in the same way.

Bandura (1977) explains that people learn new behaviors by observing and imitating others, especially those they respect or identify with. Sometimes, your empowered choices plant seeds that take years to bloom. A single act of courage—a boundary set, a dream pursued, a truth spoken—can inspire someone else in ways you may never see. Your courage becomes a silent invitation for others to step onto their own pedestals, to rewrite their stories, and to pursue lives of authenticity and fulfillment.

The ripple effect extends beyond inspiration. Empowered individuals naturally lift up those around them. As the Pedestal Philosophy explains, when you are deeply rooted in your own self-worth, you feel less threatened by others' success or happiness. You become more generous with your encouragement, more open to teamwork, and more willing to mentor or support others on their paths. Empowerment, in this sense, is not a limited resource. The more you give, the more it grows.

However, the journey is not without challenges. Resistance is unavoidable. Not everyone will understand or support your decision to step onto your pedestal. Some might feel threatened, uneasy, or even critical. This is a natural part of the ripple effect. True empowerment often questions the status quo and unsettles those invested in old patterns. The Pedestal Philosophy reminds us that your worth does not depend on others' approval. The ripples you create are most powerful when they are based on authenticity and integrity.

To sustain the ripple effect, empowered individuals must continue to nurture themselves. Self-care, reflection, and ongoing learning are essential for personal growth. It is easy to become depleted when giving to others, but empowerment flourishes when it is replenished. This is not selfishness, but stewardship, ensuring that the well runs deep enough to nourish both the self and the community.

The ripple effect of empowerment is a testament to the interconnectedness of human experience. Each empowered choice, no matter how small, sends out waves that touch lives in unexpected ways. You may never know the full impact of your actions, but rest assured that they matter. By climbing onto your own pedestal and living with authenticity, you permit others to do the same.

In the end, empowerment is not just a personal achievement; it is a collective gift. It is the spark that ignites hope, the hand that lifts another, the voice that breaks the silence. The world needs your courage, your vision, and your willingness to create ripples of change. As you empower yourself, you empower others, and together, you shape a future where everyone has the opportunity to rise.

Chapter 17

The Legacy of the Pedestal Philosophy

E very philosophy that endures leaves its mark not only on those who practice it, but also on the world around them. The Pedestal Philosophy is no exception. Its legacy is measured not just in personal transformation but in the cultural shift and ripple effects it inspires across generations. To speak of legacy is to speak of impact, continuity, and how an idea becomes a living force, long after its first spark.

The Pedestal Philosophy began as a quiet revolution. An invitation to reclaim self-worth, authenticity, and personal power. It was never about building walls of superiority, but about stepping into self-recognition, self-respect, and self-leadership. Each person is encouraged to build and stand on their own pedestal, not as a throne above others, but as a foundation for living with intention and integrity.

The most significant legacy is the internal change that occurs when someone chooses to value themselves. This journey of learning to trust intuition, set boundaries, and live by one's principles creates a quiet confidence that no external situation can shake. It is not a fleeting sense of power, but a deep-rooted belief in one's own worth and potential. These internal shifts become evident in relationships. When individuals honor their own needs and values, they bring greater authenticity and presence into every connection. Relationships, whether personal or professional, become more honest and fulfilling, built on mutual respect rather than dependency or sacrifice.

As this change unfolds, it reaches beyond the individual. Families become spaces where each member is encouraged to find and honor their own pedestal. Children raised in such environments learn early that their voices matter, their boundaries are respected, and their dreams are worth pursuing. In workplaces, this mindset fosters cultures of respect, collaboration, and innovation. Empowered employees bring their authentic selves to work, fueling creativity and resilience within teams.

The Pedestal Philosophy challenges societal norms by offering a countercultural message: real fulfillment comes not from meeting external expectations, but from aligning life with inner truth. This message is especially vital during times of rapid change or uncertainty, when traditional models of success or happiness fall short. The philosophy serves as a compass, guiding individuals back to themselves when the world feels overwhelming.

A key part of the Pedestal Philosophy's legacy is its flexibility. It is not rigid or prescriptive, but encourages ongoing reflection and adjustment. Each person's pedestal is unique, shaped by their experiences, values, and goals. The philosophy invites people to revisit and rebuild their pedestal as they grow, ensuring it remains relevant and approachable across cultures, generations, and changing circumstances.

The legacy is also carried forward in the stories that are shared. Every time someone tells of reclaiming their power, setting a boundary, or living authentically, they add another thread to the tapestry of the Pedestal Philosophy. These stories offer inspiration and hope to others just starting their journey and remind us that transformation is possible, even when the odds seem insurmountable.

Education and mentorship play a vital role in passing down the legacy. Those who embody the Pedestal Philosophy naturally support others on their journeys. As teachers, coaches, parents, or friends, they live with self-respect and authenticity, modeling what it means to build and ascend one's own pedestal. The philosophy is shared not through rigid rules, but through example and encouragement.

Communities built on self-respect, mutual support, and shared values become collective forces for change. When individuals come together, each firmly on their own pedestal, they are better prepared to face challenges, celebrate diversity, and encourage innovation. Empowered individuals form the foundation of empowered communities, shaping institutions and movements that prioritize well-being, equity, and genuine leadership.

The Pedestal Philosophy also redefines success. Rather than measuring achievement by wealth, status, or external validation, it emphasizes fulfillment, integrity, and impact. People are inspired to define success in ways that reflect their own values and goals, allowing for greater diversity in what is celebrated and pursued.

As the philosophy spreads, its legacy becomes intergenerational. Parents who practice the Pedestal Philosophy pass on not just advice, but living examples of self-honor. They raise children who are resilient and self-aware, capable of navigating life's complexities with confidence. These children grow up to adapt and carry the philosophy forward, connecting past, present, and future through ongoing self-leadership and authenticity.

On a broader scale, as more people embrace the Pedestal Philosophy, cultural conversations shift. Discussions about self-worth, boundaries, and authenticity become more accepted. There is less stigma around seeking support or changing paths, and a greater focus on reflection, growth, and learning from mistakes. This cultural shift opens space for compassion, understanding, and collective progress.

Perhaps the most enduring legacy of the Pedestal Philosophy is the profound sense of hope it instills. In a world that often leaves us feeling fragmented or isolated, the philosophy offers a vision of wholeness and renewal. It assures us that no matter how lost or disconnected we may feel, we are never truly alone. There is always a way to return to ourselves, a pedestal waiting to be reclaimed and rebuilt. This hope is not naive optimism, but a resilient force that helps us navigate life's inevitable ups and downs with grace and courage. Every setback can be a prelude to growth, and every period of doubt an opportunity to rediscover our strength.

As the Pedestal Philosophy is practiced and passed down, it becomes a living legacy—one shaped by every person who chooses to honor their worth and support others on their journey. The philosophy endures not in theory, but in daily choices: speaking truth, setting boundaries, pursuing dreams, and uplifting others. Its legacy is dynamic, growing with every empowered individual and every community that chooses authenticity and intention.

You are now part of this living legacy. The world will always offer reasons to shrink or seek validation elsewhere, but your pedestal is yours to claim, shape, and share. Let your journey be a beacon for others, a testament to the strength that comes from self-leadership and authenticity. Carry this philosophy forward: celebrate your growth, honor your truth, and invite others to do the same.

The legacy of the Pedestal Philosophy is alive in you. Pass it on boldly, and let it shape not just your life, but the world around you—one empowered choice at a time.

A Call to Courage

If you have made it here, you already know this journey is not about perfection or having all the answers. It is about choosing, every day, to honor your own story—even when it is messy, unfinished, or uncertain. The Pedestal Philosophy is not just a framework; it is a living practice, and now, it belongs to you.

You have seen how cracks can appear, how setbacks can shake your confidence, and how easily you can forget your own worth. But you have also seen what happens when you choose to rebuild, to listen to your intuition, and to stand in your own light. That is courage—not the absence of fear, but the willingness to show up for yourself, again and again.

So here is my invitation: Let your next act of courage be something small and personal. Maybe it is saying yes to a dream you have shelved, or saying no to a pattern that no longer serves you. Maybe it is sharing your truth with someone, or simply looking in the mirror and offering yourself kindness. Let your courage be a quiet, daily commitment to stay on your pedestal, even when it feels easier to step down.

Remember, you do not walk this path alone. Every time you choose yourself, you give others permission to do the same. Your story—honest, imperfect, and authentic—is powerful. Trust it. Let it guide you.

This is your pedestal. Stand tall, and let the world see who you truly are.

Reflection and Action Guide

This workbook section is designed to help you put the Pedestal Philosophy into practice. Use these prompts and exercises to reflect, take action, and track your growth. You can write directly in these pages, use a separate journal (recommended), and revisit the exercises as often as you need.

1. The Foundation of the Pedestal Philosophy

Prompt:

What beliefs about self-worth did you inherit from your family, culture, or early experiences?

Which of these beliefs do you want to keep, and which do you want to let go?

Exercise:

Write a letter to your younger self, affirming the worth and value you wish you had always known.

2. Loving Yourself First

Prompt:

List three ways you currently show love to yourself.

1)

2)

3)

What is one small act of self-kindness you can practice this week?

Exercise:

Create a "self-love menu"—a list of activities or rituals that help you recharge and feel cared for.

3. The Art of Self-Discovery

Prompt:

What are your top five personal values?

1)

2)

3)

4)

5)

When do you feel most like your authentic self?

Exercise:

Try something new this month that aligns with your values—journal about what you learned from the experience.

4. Authenticity and Inner Validation

Prompt:

When was the last time you acted out of alignment with your true self? How did it feel?

What would it look like to validate yourself instead of seeking approval?

Exercise:

Write an "authenticity intention" for the next week: one way you will honor your truth in daily life.

5. Shattering the Illusion of External Pedestals

Prompt:

Who, if anyone, have you placed on a pedestal? Has someone done this to you?

How has this dynamic impacted your self-worth or relationships?

Exercise:

Reflect on a time you sought external validation. What did you need in that moment, and how can you give it to yourself now?

6. The Journey Through Pain

Prompt:

What pain, loss, or disappointment has shaped you most?

What did you learn about yourself through that experience?

Exercise:

Write about a painful experience using the "three lessons" method: What happened, what you felt, and what you learned.

7. The Strength in Vulnerability

Prompt:

When have you risked being vulnerable? What was the outcome?

What is one area of your life where you would like to be more open?

Exercise:

Share a truth about yourself with someone you trust, or write it in your journal if you are not ready to share aloud.

8. Relationships and the Pedestal

Prompt:

Which relationships support your pedestal, and which challenge it?

Where do you need to set a new boundary or have an honest conversation?

Exercise:

Map your support circle. Who uplifts you? Who drains you? What changes do you want to make?

9. The Courage to Stand in Your Truth

Prompt:

When was the last time you stood up for yourself? What did you learn?

What truth do you need to speak, and to whom?

Exercise:

Draft a script for a courageous conversation you need to have—even if you never send it.

10. Reclaiming Your Power

Prompt:

Where in your life have you given away your power?

What is one step you can take to reclaim it?

Exercise:

List three things you can say "no" to this week to honor your energy and priorities.

1)

2)

3)

11. Building Your Pedestal

Prompt:

What does your ideal pedestal look like? What qualities or beliefs is it built on?

Exercise:

Draw or describe your pedestal. List the foundational beliefs, values, and practices you want to reinforce.

12. Climbing on Your Pedestal

Prompt:

What is holding you back from claiming your space?

What would it feel like to "climb on your pedestal" today?

Exercise:

Set a "visibility goal" for the week—one way you will show up more boldly in your life or work.

13. Setbacks and Rebuilding: When Your Pedestal Cracks

Prompt:

Describe a recent setback. What did you feel? What did you learn?

How did you (or how could you) begin to rebuild?

Exercise:

Write a letter of encouragement to yourself for the next time you face a setback.

14. Controlling Your Balance

Prompt:

Where do you feel out of balance in your life at the moment?

Exercise:

Choose one area (work, relationships, self-care, etc.) and set a realistic goal to restore balance.

15. The Ripple Effect of Empowerment

Prompt:

Who has been empowered by your journey? Who inspires you?

Exercise: Reach out to someone you admire or mentor someone who could benefit from your experience.

16. The Legacy of the Pedestal Philosophy

Prompt:

What legacy do you want to leave for your family, community, or the world?

Exercise: Write a short legacy statement or letter to your future self or loved ones.

17. A Call to Courage

Prompt:

What does courage look like for you today?

Exercise: Set an intention for one courageous act you will take this week, no matter how small.

Bonus:

Monthly Check-In: At the end of each month, revisit your reflections and actions. What has changed? Where have you grown? What new intentions do you want to set?

Acknowledgments

To Kim, you are an extraordinary woman and dear friend whom I regard as family. Thank you for always beta-reading not just my books but also the concepts from the moment I start drafting chapter ideas. You are a true gem.

To my boss-girl sister tribe. Blessed to break the myth that women of color cannot boldly and fiercely support one another, love one another, and respect one another in masses (no matter where we are in our life journeys): Tameaka Roundtree, Denise Turner, Tasani Butcher, Ashley McGirt-Adair, Dr. Cortina Louis, Diana Richardson-Phillipus, Tammy Reese, Viliane Bazile, Janay Scott, Carmen Lewis, Maribeth Neufville, and Chavis Walker. If I missed you, please charge it to my head, not my heart.

To all the women who have struggled with their autonomy, who have faced painful experiences and risen above them—you are seen, honored, and celebrated.

To all the victors and overcomers, the women who have reclaimed their power and chosen to live authentically, unapologetically, and courageously: your strength, resilience, and determination inspire me and countless others. May you continue to climb to your pedestal and stand tall in your truth.

About the Author

D r. Pamela Gurley is a world-renowned author, speaker, and passionate literacy advocate who believes in the transformative power of words. As the founder of Clark and Hill Enterprise, IAMDRPGURLEY, and the Brown Girl and Brown Boy Literacy Foundation, she dedicates her work to empowering children and adults to find their voice, embrace their stories, and break barriers through education.

With a Doctorate in Management and a background in psychology and administration, Dr. Gurley brings both expertise and lived experience to her mission. Her initiatives—including the Brown Girl and Brown Boy Kid's Red-Carpet Book Tour and the Literacy Festival—have inspired thousands and sparked meaningful change in communities nationwide.

Beyond her advocacy, Dr. Gurley is known for her authenticity and her ability to connect with audiences of all ages. Whether she is hosting the Herspiration Happy Hour podcast, leading a workshop, or writing her next book, she shows up as her whole self: relatable, driven, and unapologetically real.

Dr. Gurley's journey is proof that you can rewrite your story at any stage of life. Her mission is simple: to help others stand tall in their truth and live a life of purpose *on purpose*.

Also By Dr. Pamela Gurley

I am Not a Stereotype: I Am H.E.R.

Bl@ck Girl Activist: Changing the Narrative of Black Women

The PR Prep Guide: 7 Critical Need-To-Know Basics Before Hiring a Publicist

Bl@ck Girl Activist: A Shift in Social Change (Anthology)

The Dream is in Her Hands: She Can Do It (Anthology)

Children's Books:

English:

Brown Boy Be Social

Brown Girl, Be Social

Brown Girl, Break Barriers

Brown Boy, Break Barriers

Brown Girl, and Brown Boy, Be Well

Brown Girl and Brown Boy, Be Mindful

Brown Girl and Brown Boy, We Love Hobbies

Brown Girl and Brown Boy, Africa Adventures

Brown Girl and Brown Boy Presents Kofi Roux the Yorkiepoo

Spanish:

Niña Morena, Sé Sociable

Niño Moreno, Sé Sociable

Niña Morena, Rompe Barreras

Niño Moreno, Rompe Barreras

Niña Morena y Niño Moreno, Manténganse Saludables

Niña Morena y Niño Moreno, Sean Considerables

Niña Morena y Niño Moreno, Nos Encantan Los Pasatiempos

French:

Petite Fille Noire, Sois Sociable

Petit Garçon Noir, Sois Sociable

Petit Garçon Noir, Brises Barrières

Petite Fille Noire, Brises Barrières

Petite Fille Noire et Petit Garçon Noir, Soyez Prévenants

Petite Fille Noire et Petit Garçon Noir, Allez Bien!

Petite Fille Noire et Petit Garçon Noir, Nous Aimons des Loisirs

References

Angelou, M. (2009). Letter to My Daughter. Random House.

Beck, J. S. (2011). Cognitive behavior therapy: Basics and beyond (2nd ed.). New York, NY: Guilford Press.

Brown, B. (2012). Daring Greatly: How the Courage to Be Vulnerable Transforms the Way We Live, Love, Parent, and Lead. Gotham Books.

Deci, E. L., & Ryan, R. M. (1985). Intrinsic Motivation and Self-Determination in Human Behavior.

Deci, E. L., & Ryan, R. M. (2000). The "what" and "why" of goal pursuits: Human needs and the self-determination of behavior. Psychological Inquiry, 11(4), 227–268.

Duckworth, A. (2016). Grit: The Power of Passion and Perseverance

Dweck, C. S. (2006). Mindset: The new psychology of success. New York, NY: Random House.

Falk, R. F., & Miller, N. B. (1998). The reflexive self: A sociological perspective. Roeper Review, 20(3), 150-153.

Forman, G. (2009). If I stay. Dutton Books.

Hemphill, P. (2020). On boundaries. [Self-published or online resource].

Hooks, B. (2000). All About Love: New Visions. William Morrow and Company.

James, W. (1890). The Principles of Psychology.

Kabat-Zinn, J. (1990). Full Catastrophe Living: Using the Wisdom of Your Body and Mind to Face Stress, Pain, and Illness

Kaur, R. (2017). *The sun and her flowers*. Andrews McMeel Publishing.

Lazarus, R. S., & Folkman, S. (1984). Stress, appraisal, and coping. New York, NY: Springer.

Leary, M. R., Tambor, E. S., Terdal, S. K., & Downs, D. L. (1995*). Self-Esteem as an Interpersonal Monitor: The Sociometer Hypothesis.*

Maslow, A. H. (1943). *A Theory of Human Motivation.*

Neff, K. (2003). *Self-Compassion: An Alternative Conceptualization of a Healthy Attitude Toward Oneself.*

Neely, M. E., Mohammed, S. S., & Roberts, R. M. (2009). Self-kindness when facing stress: The role of self-compassion, goal regulation, and support in college students' well-being. Motivation and Emotion, 33(1), 88–97.

Perel, E. (2017). *The State of Affairs: Rethinking Infidelity.* Harper.

Rogers, C. (1961). **On Becoming a Person: A Therapist's View of Psychotherapy**

Rosen, L. D., Lim, A. F., Carrier, L. M., & Cheever, N. A. (2011). An Empirical Examination of the Educational Impact of Text Message-Induced Task Switching in the Classroom: Educational Implications and Strategies to Enhance Learning. Educational Psychology, 31(8), 993–1019.

Ryan, R. M., & Deci, E. L. (2000). Self-determination theory and the facilitation of intrinsic motivation, social development, and well-being. American Psychologist, 55(1), 68–78.

Snyder, C. R., Maddux, J. E., & Baron, K. E. (2012). Handbook of self-esteem theory and research. New York, NY: Guilford Press.

Tedeschi, R. G., & Calhoun, L. G. (2004). *Posttraumatic Growth: Conceptual Foundations and Empirical Evidence*

Wong, C. C. Y., & Yeung, N. C. Y. (2017). Self-compassion and posttraumatic growth: Cognitive processes as mediators. Mindfulness, 8(4), 1078–1087.

www.ingramcontent.com/pod-product-compliance
Lightning Source LLC
Chambersburg PA
CBHW051522120626
46551CB00012B/1038